AF556054

BABA BANDA SINGH BAHADUR

BABA BANDA SINGH BAHADUR

Battle Strategy against Mughal Forces

Dr. Surinder Singh

HAR-ANAND
PUBLICATIONS PVT LTD

HAR-ANAND PUBLICATIONS PVT LTD
E-49/3, Okhla Industrial Area, Phase-II, New Delhi-110020
Tel.: 41603490
E-mail: info@haranandbooks.com/haranand@rediffmail.com
Shop online at: www.haranandbooks.com

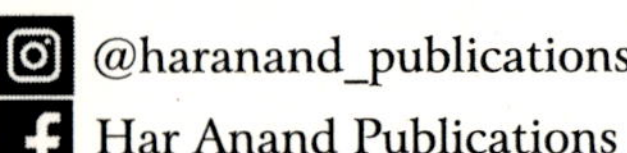

Reprint, 2025

Published by Ashok Gosain and Ashish Gosain for
Har-Anand Publications Pvt Ltd

Printed in India at Royal Press

Preface

To control the Hazara tribals a small town called Haripur was raised by Hari Singh Nalwa, the bravest commander of the Khalsa army in early 19th century. I have lived there the initial 18 years of my life (1929 to 1947) in a dream world of my own. When the partition of the country took place with great upheaval, our family had to move to the Indian side. My university education got fairly disturbed. I was, however, able to complete my studies, although belatedly and was selected in the Indian Defence Accounts Service.

A little over thirty years of lack lustre service of Defence Accounts was completed in 1987. During the later part of my service I took to sculpture, as a hobby, from drift wood, high density polythene waste and iron scrap collected from army firing ranges. My first sculpture from metal scrap was a bust of a Madras Sapper which I made in an army workshop has been gifted to the MEG Centre, Bangalore where it has been installed at the main door of the Museum. I also developed an interest in coin collection. An inner admonition restricted my interest to the collection and study of Sikh coins only.

After my retirement, I settled down in Chandigarh and started studying the legends etc on the Sikh coins in my collection. Although Sikh coinage has been the youngest medieval Indian state currency 1710-13 and 1765-1849 there is very little record thereof available in libraries, Museums and archives. Historians who have mentioned Sikh coins in their accounts have done so without any actual examination of these coins and the explanations of the legends given by most of them are not correct. The Sikh coinage issued by Banda Bahadur (1710-13) is perhaps the finest in the world of coinage in its depiction of the concepts of Sikh Sovereignty.

My study appeared like joining a primary school afresh, but with no class room, no teacher, no examination and all by myself. The redeeming feature being that, it gave me satisfaction with a purpose to my liking. To understand various aspects of Sikh coins, I had to study Sikh history in detail from Guru period to the decline and fall of Sikh state. As and when I could locate some useful reference thereto, it would give me great joy for days together. It was a very peculiar race, in which there was no competitor, no starter, no judge, no end in sight and only passage of time would raise uneasiness in me about its completion.

The study of coinage is an altogether different subject from the collection of coins. Huge stocks of coins collected by individuals are lying unexplored and have no useful purpose other than their monetary value.

Whichever aspect of Sikh coinage I could resolve, I presented the same in the form of research papers at the three universities of Punjab and Indian History Conference. I could not get a guide for Ph. D from any of the universities in Punjab. Finally, I did my Ph. D from Rabindra Bharati University, Calcutta in 2000-2001. I converted my research thesis "Studies in Sikh Coinage" into a book form "Sikh Coinage: Symbol of Sikh Sovereignty" which was published in 2004. It has been well received and is deemed a reference book for coins collectors and research scholars.

Banda Bahadur was the first to issue Sikh coinage and I had to study the life and achievements of Banda Bahadur in various aspects of war-craft and State-craft which has left a very deep imprint on my mind. Banda Bahadur had taken up on himself an unequal fight with the Mughal governors and even with the Mughal emperors. Mughal forces had all the advantages of large, well-equipped and well-trained armies duly supported with sufficient stocks of food, arms and ammunition and unlimited finances. Banda Bahadur's volunteer force had only an unbounded spirit to carry on the fight initiated by their 10th Master. They had, to a great extent, conquered the fear of death, otherwise they were very short in numbers, ill-equipped and untrained, with very little food and war materials. Banda Bahadur used indigenous tactics to offset the numerical advantage of enemy forces. Banda Bahadur would initially watch the battle from a vantage point and if a section of his troops came under great pressure, he would join them. In no time he would literally bring about a change in the situation and lead them to success.

It is a great irony that the Indian nation, the Punjabis and Sikhs in particular, for whom Banda Bahadur made such a great contribution have literally disowned him while his contributions entitle him to the first rank of commanders the world over by any standards. My effort is to bring out the greatness of Banda Bahadur which has been clouded by historians seemingly inimical to him for frivolous and unfounded reasons. I have been virtually living with Banda Bahadur for the past couple of years and strongly feel that the nation owes a debt of gratitude towards him and in all fairness should give him his due place under the Sun.

During the initial years of 18th century, in spite of Mughal Government's all out efforts to literally wipe out the Sikhs with all sorts of barbaric atrocities and executions, Banda Bahadur has made a phenomenal contribution to keep the flame of Sikh existence alive and burning. The subject of battle strategies of Banda Bahadur does not seem to have been dealt with earlier and this seems to be first attempt on this subject.

I am obliged to Prof. G. S. Randhawa, ex-VC, Guru Nanak Dev University, Amritsar and Maj Gen Kuldip Singh Bajwa for their assistance and encouragement.

DR. SURINDER SINGH

CONTENTS

"A wise man of learning in Israel once said that there is no end to the writing of books. Adding one more would therefore be pointless, unless it broke fresh ground."

Lewis Browne in *Wisdom of Israel*

These words weighed very heavily on my mind when I considered the desirability of getting this book published. I believe that my study does break fresh ground and reveals authentic historical appreciation regarding the battle strategies of Banda Bahadur, a subject matter which does not appear to have been attempted by historians as such till date.

Dr. Surinder Singh

I

Introduction

Prince Mauzam, on hearing of the death of Aurangzeb rushed from Kabul and declared himself Emperor under the title Bahadur Shah and reached Delhi on 20th May, 1707. There being no law of primogeniture among Muslim rulers, Azam, the second son of Aurangzeb, captured the Mughal treasury and moved towards Delhi to claim Emperorship. Guru Gobind Singh was staying at Delhi in a "mochi colony" now named as Motibagh. With the intervention of some mutual associates Guru ji agreed to send a few hundred of his horsemen under the command of Bhai Dharam Singh to support Bahadur Shah against Azam at the battle fought at Jajau on 8th June 1707 in which Azam along with his principal officers was defeated and killed. Bahadur Shah invited Guru Gobind Singh while at Agra, Guru ji and his armed men were received and various presents exchanged between them as a thanksgiving for Guru ji's timely assistance.

Guruji approached Bahadur Shah to punish Wazir Khan, *faujdar* of Sirhind, for the execution of his young sons. Bahadur Shah was delaying the matter when news came of Kam Baksh's rebellion at Hyderabad. Bahadur Shah requested Guru ji to come with him and Guru ji moved with the Emperor in the hope of securing a punishment for Wazir Khan. While at Nander Guru ji understood Bahadur Shah's evasiveness and set up his camp on the bank of river Godawari at Nander and the emperor moved towards Hyderabad.

At Nander, Guru ji met Madho Dass Bairagi, and converted him to Sikhism, named him Banda Singh Bahadur and sent him to Panjab to lead the Sikhs in their fight against Mughal tyranny. Guru ji also sent five senior Sikhs as his advisers and about 20 troops and some gifts of his personal arms to Banda Bahadur. Banda Bahadur left for Panjab in October 1708 and going by circuitous routes to avoid detection by elaborate Mughal spy system, he reached Kharkhauda, 30 kms short of Delhi around September 1709.

Banda Bahadur fought over twenty battles with Mughal forces under Mughal commanders and some even under direct command of the Mughal emperors. In all these battles, Mughal forces were far superior, in numbers, artillery, arms ammunition, food-stocks and replacement of men and materials. Whereas the Sikh forces were less in man power, untrained and ill-equipped volunteer force, always running short of ammunition and food stocks. They were, however, able to win many battles and hold their own against the Mughal forces. The victories of the Sikh forces have been due to death-defying bravery of the men and battle tactics adopted by their commander Banda Bahadur.

While incidentally, going through books on Business Administration, I saw Sun Tzu's Classic books 'The Art of War' and 'The Art of Strategy' and a couple of more such books and came to know that all institutions of management and even the army organizations study these books for purposes of assistance in effective struggle for supremacy. These books were located in 1772 by a French Jesuit P. Amiot who translated them in

French and presented to Napoleon Bonaparte. N. Conard translated these books in Russian and the same have been used in Russian wars. Captain E.F. Calthrop translated these in English. These books became very popular with the generals of the western world and soon became a subject of management institutes all over the world.

After studying these books, I felt that the strategy worked by Banda Bahadur and by the Chinese experts of those times (AD 618-906) were, to a great extent, similar to each other, e.g., the morale of the soldiers and the surprise element of the attack were two major items in battle strategies.

Mahabharata, the epic war of India, and to certain extent Kautilya's *Arthshastra* throw light on the art of war and the battle strategies. Since these are mixed with fables and fiction, the same have not been viewed as guiding principles. Banda Bahadur's application of strategy in wars fought hardly 300 years back with all the actual details of those battles being available, are far more useful than the Chinese Sun Tzu's Classic which are in the short form of rules and wanting in details of the battles. In this book the details of the battles and the exposition of the battle strategies are given in a continuous form for the better appreciation of the situation and the strategy. I am of the considered opinion that study of Banda Bahadur's battle strategies should be given a place in the study of battle strategies by the Institutes of Management and the Defence organizations and their institutions for study by their officers and men.

II

Banda Singh Bahadur—A Profile

After the demise of Guru Gobind Singh on 7th October, 1708, the Sikhs soon developed into a political power under the leadership of Banda Bahadur who came to Panjab, not as Guru but as the commander of the Khalsa.[1] Before Banda Bahadur's departure from the Deccan the Guru bestowed upon him a drum and a flag as emblems of temporal authority and five arrows from his own quiver. He was blessed with victory provided he considered himself to be a comrade, a servant of the Khalsa and with whom would rest the supreme authority of the community. Leading five Sikhs, Binod Singh, Kahan Singh, Baj Singh, Daya Singh and Ram Singh, accompanied Banda Bahadur to Panjab to be of assistance to him in his mission against the Mughal rulers.[2]

Arriving in northern India Banda Singh dispatched the *hukamnamas* of Guru Gobind Singh to prominent Sikhs in Panjab. His main target, to begin with, was Wazir Khan, the *faujdar* of Sirhind, the killer of Guru Gobind Singh's young sons.[3] The cold-blooded murder of the innocent children of the Guru had given the Sikhs a shock and they were burning with rage against him. The leading Sikhs of the Panjab, Bhai Fateh

[1]Payne C.H., *A Short History of Sikhs,* London, p. 43.

[2]Ganda Singh, *Banda Singh Bahadur,* Amritsar, 1935, pp. 24-25.

[3]Bhangoo Rattan Singh, *Prachin Panth Parkash,* 1939, p. 72.

Singh, Karam Singh, Dharam Singh, Nagahia Singh, Aali Singh and Mali Singh, flocked round him along with their followers. According to Khafi Khan, within two to three months, four to five thousand horsemen and seven to eight thousand foot-soldiers joined him and their number soon rose to 40,000.[4]

Places like Samana, Gurham, Thaska and Shahabad fell without resistance. The battle against Wazir Khan of Sirhind, the murderer of the younger sons of Guru Gobind Singh was fought on the plain of Chappar-Chiri (actual name being Chhapparh Jhiri) on May 12, 1710, and he was killed. The Khalsa flag was hoisted on the fort of Sirhind.[5] Baj Singh, the leader of the Trans-Satluj Sikhs, was appointed governor of Sirhind, with Aali Singh, the leader of the Cis-Satluj Sikhs as his deputy.[6] Fateh Singh was made the governor of Samana and Ram Singh was posted to Thanesar as its governor jointly with Binod Singh.[7] More than 200 years after the battle of Sirhind, it is reported that so great was the feeling of revenge among the Sikhs against Wazir Khan that railway train would stop for a few minutes opposite Sirhind fort and passengers would rush to pick up a couple of bricks and throw them in the river as token of their contribution in the destruction of Sirhind.

As the Sikhs had been feeling very sore about Wazir Khan's role in the harassment of Guru Gobind Singh, their action at Sirhind was evidently instigated by a spirit of revenge. But the Muslim writers have given highly exaggerated accounts of the Sikhs. "The *Siyar-ul-Mutakhrin* and also the *Muntakhab-ul-*

[4]Khafi Khan, *Muntakhab-ul-Lubab*, Vol. II, p. 652.

[5]Karam Singh, *Banda Bahadur*, p. 77.

[6]*Ibid.*, p. 87.

[7]Narang G.C., *Transformation of Sikhism*, Lahore, 1912, p. 107.

Lubab contain terrible details of the deeds of atrocities by the Sikhs," writes Thornton "but a Muhammadan writer is not to be implicitly trusted upon such a point."[8] Later writers like Mohammad Latif have blindly followed the statements of Ghulam Husain Khan and Khafi Khan.

Banda Bahadur was told that Jalal Khan and Ali Hamid Khan, the *faujdars* of Deoband and Saharanpur, were harassing the Sikh converts there. He repaired to that part of the country and addressed a letter to Jalal Khan to release the Sikhs who had been taken prisoners by him and submit to the authority of the Khalsa.[9] Sikh messengers were mounted on asses and turned out of the town.[10] Jalalabad and Saharanpur were, therefore, attacked. The Sikhs were reinforced by the Gujjar peasants who had suffered long at the hands of the Sheikhzadas of Saharanpur.[11] It assumed the form of a class struggle with tenants on one side and the *zamindars* on the other. In the bloody fighting about three hundred Sheikhzadas fell dead in the court-yard of Sheikh Muhammad Afzal alone.

Now the Sikhs addressed a letter to Shamas Khan, the *faujdar* of Jullundur, calling upon him to effect some reforms and to personally hand over his treasury to the Khalsa. In reply he declared a *jehad* or crusade against the Sikhs.[12] The Sikhs had about forty to fifty thousand horse and foot. No doubt in the

[8]Thornton, *History of Panjab*, Allen and Co, 1846, Vol. I, p. 176.

[9]Ganda Singh, *Banda Singh Bahadur, op. cit.*, p. 80.

It was the practice with Banda Bahadur to inform the ruler of the place, that he proposed to proceed against, to accept his allegiance. In the case of a negative reply, he considered himself justified to make an assault.

[10]Irvine William, *Later Mughals*, Vol. I, pp. 101-02.

[11]Ganda Singh, *Banda Singh Bahadur, op. cit.*, p. 95.

[12]Khafi Khan, *Muntakhab-ul-Lubab*, Vol. II, p. 658.

flush of victory a large number of Hindus also joined the forces of Banda Bahadur to reap the benefits and enjoy the fruits of the success over their Mughal masters. Many of the spirited and daring Hindus adopted Sikhism.[13] After a few days the Muslims dispersed and the Sikhs got an easy control over Jullundur and Hoshiarpur. This was done during the last quarter of the year 1710. Banda Singh then turned his attention to Batala and Kalanaur and some other Sikh leaders occupied the *pargana* of Pathankot.[14] There was by now, no noble-man daring enough to march from Delhi against them.[15]

Emperor Bahadur Shah hastily quitted Deccan to attend to the Sikh insurgency in the north. On 8th September, 1710, the Emperor issued an order that "All Hindus employed in the imperial offices should have their beards shaved."[16] Again on 10th December, 1710, the Emperor issued an edict ordering a wholesale genocide of the Sikhs the worshippers of Nanak wherever found. This order was later repeated by Emperor Farrukh Siyar in almost the same words.

Banda Bahadur did establish a new state, no doubt, but he ruled not in his own name but in the name of the *Khalsa* and the *Gurus*. According to Rattan Singh Bhangu, "The Guru had enjoined upon Banda to serve the *Panth*. And it was not he but the collective Sikh community that was blessed with the sovereignty by the *Sacha Padshah* (Guru Gobind Singh).[17] Banda Bahadur proved equal to the responsibility entrusted to him and he abided by his master's instructions.

[13]Karam Singh, *Banda Bahadur, op. cit.*, p. 122.

[14]Khafi Khan, *op. cit.*, Vol. II, p. 680.

[15]Ganda Singh, *Banda Bahadur, op. cit.*, p. 122.

[16]Ganda Singh, *Banda Singh Bahadur, op. cit.*, p. 128.

[17]Bhangoo Rattan Singh, *Prachin Panth Prakash, op. cit.*, p. 117.

In his letter of 12th December, 1710, addressed to the Sikhs of Jaunpur, Banda Bahadur wrote, "The Guru will protect you. Call upon the Guru's name. On seeing the letter come to my presence, wearing five arms. Observe the rules of conduct laid down for the Khalsa.... We have to bring about the golden age (*satya yuga*). Love one another. This is my wish. He who lives according to the rules of the Khalsa shall be saved by the Guru."[18]

This letter gives the important features of the Sikh Polity adopted by Banda Bahadur presumably on the directions given to him by Guru Gobind Singh. He strongly recommends that the conduct of the Sikhs, the Khalsa, in the liberated country, was to be in strict conformity with the principles laid down by Guru Gobind Singh at the time of their initiation ceremony into the order of the Khalsa. He pointed out that the golden age had been ushered in. He meant to tell the people at large that a welfare state of their dreams had been established to the exclusion of the tyrannical government of the Mughal governors. He tacitly meant to convey to them that unjust officials had been substituted by the just, deserving and competent persons who could appreciate the aspirations of the oppressed and the harassed people.

One measure which influenced the future fiscal history of the Punjab was the liquidation of the *zamindari* system. The Mughal *zamindars* or landlords were responsible for the payment of fixed amount of land revenue from the villages entrusted to them. They extorted from the peasants any amount they liked and the government did not interfere, with the result that the poor farmers were reduced to the position of mere slaves. On Banda

[18] *Hukamnama* (Ganda Singh edited), No. 67, p. 195.

Bahadur's suggestion the tillers of soil ejected the landlords and the peasants themselves became the master of their lands. Large estates were broken into smaller holdings in the hands of the Sikh or Hindu peasants. These agrarian changes to a great extent ameliorated the lot of the poor peasantry.[19]

With victory coming to the Sikhs, they began to be looked upon as defenders of the faith and the protectors of the land. Banda Bahadur's brief rule gave the Sikhs a foretaste of independence and from that time onwards they could not be satisfied with anything short of the wresting of their territory from the Mughal yoke, in pursuit of which they launched a ceaseless struggle against the Mughal government of the Punjab.

William Irvine saying that, "in all the *parganas* occupied by the Sikhs the reversal of the previous customs was striking and complete. A low scavenger or leather dresser, the lowest of the low in Indian estimation had only to leave home and join the Guru (meaning Banda) when in a short time he would return to his birth-place as its ruler with his order of appointment in his hand. As soon as he set foot within the boundaries the well-born and wealthy went out to greet him and escort him home. Arrived there, they stood before him with joined palms, awaiting his orders. Not a soul dared to disobey an order and men who had often risked themselves in battle-field became so cowed down that they were afraid even to remonstrate.[20]

Banda Bahadur had converted a large number of Hindus and Muslims to Sikhism but he does not seem to have used any force to propagate his religion. Some people might have joined the Sikh fold to escape punishment for their former misdeeds or to

[19]Bhagat Singh, *Panjab Past and Present*, October 1984, Vol. XVIII-II p. 10.
[20]Irvine William, *Later Mughals, op. cit.*, Vol. I, pp. 98-99.

safeguard their prospects of livelihood. Throughout the history of the Sikhs it has been a glowing feature of the polity of various rulers to adopt a non-communal and tolerant policy towards those who agreed to be their subjects. Banda Singh was no exception to it. When he reached Kalanaur from Bahrampur, the Muslims of Kalanaur paid allegiance to him and joined his forces. This seems to be the result of religious toleration shown to the Muslim population of the place.

A similar reference was made by Amin-ud-Daulah in June 1710 that "the authority of that deluded sect (of the Sikhs) had reached such extremes that many Hindus and Muhammadan adopted their faith and ritual. Their chief (Banda Bahadur) captivated the hearts of all towards his inclinations and, whether a Hindu or a Muhammadan, whosoever came into contact with him was addressed as a Singh. Accordingly, Dindar Khan, a powerful ruler of the neighbourhood was named Dindar Singh and Mir Nasir-ud-Din, the official reporter of Sirhind, became Mir Nasir Singh. In much the same way a large number of Muhammadan abandoned Islam and followed the misguided path (of Sikhism) and took solemn oaths and firm pledges to stand by Banda."[21]

Banda Bahadur was the first to organize the Sikhs and to build a political power. He fought battles not only to weaken the Mughal power but also to replace it by a better one. He had, therefore, no alternative, but to oust the Mughal government officials, appoint his own men, introduce changes in the government set-up and adopt a polity that aimed at fulfilling the aspirations of the Sikhs.[22]

[21]Teja Singh and Ganda Singh, *A Short History of Sikhs*, p. 86.

[22]Bhagat Singh, *Panjab Past and Present, op. cit.*, p. 13.

The Sikh struggle under Banda Bahadur had strong social base in the villages. Therefore, we find a marked role of the peasants and *zamindars* in the activities of Banda Bahadur. As soon as he started his operations in the Panjab, the *zamindars* promptly put trust in him and accepted him as their leader. At the instance of the *zamindars* hundreds and thousands of others rallied around him. During the entire period of their struggle against the Mughals, Banda Bahadur and his Sikhs could move almost unchecked in the major parts of the Punjab. The *zamindars* of the Panjab, mainly of the northern districts of Bari Doab, supplied arms and horses to Banda Bahadur and many of the hill chieftains of the Shivalik areas provided him shelter following the arrival of Bahadur Shah in the Panjab and the deployment against the Sikhs of the entire Mughal army of the northern province.[23] The Sikhs had set up a few *chowkis* in the Kehlur hills so as during their fleeing nobody was able to obstruct their way. It had been again and again brought to the notice of the Emperor that most of the hill chiefs were sympathetic to Banda Bahadur and lent him every possible help.

There is no denying the fact that it was a war between the unequals. The Mughal Government had a big organized army at its command. The Mughal army was well-equipped, well-officered and well-trained but the Sikh comrades of Banda Bahadur were handicapped in many ways. They were an untrained, indisciplined and improperly equipped rabble but their shortcomings were made up by their faith in the genuineness of their cause and their long tradition of undergoing sacrifices and sufferings for a good and righteous cause.

[23] *Ibid.*, p. 14.

Banda Bahadur was largely responsible for the liquidation of the *zamindari* system in the Punjab. On his suggestion, the tillers of the soil ejected the landlords and the peasants themselves became the masters of the land. Large estates were broken into smaller holdings in the hands of Sikh or Hindu peasants. These agrarian changes, to a great extent, ameliorated the lot of the poor peasantry. He ousted the Mughal officers from the various *parganas* of Sirhind division and put his own men in their places. Hindu *qanungos* and *amils* had been replaced by Muslims under Aurangzeb. The Mughal officials were dismissed and the jobs of the displaced Hindus were restored to them.[24]

The merchants, extended their support to the Mughals. In view of their vested economic interests sometimes the urban Khatris financed the voluntary efforts of the Sayyids, etc., to fight against the Sikhs. The Khatris thus got closer to the government and got high positions under Jahandar Shah and Farrukh Siyar. Suba Chand, a mere *munshi* of Zulfiqar Khan, obtained the title of Raja from Jahandar Shah and rose to the office of *Diwan-i-Khalsa*.[25]

The author of *Asrar-i-Samadhi* (the exact name is not clearly known but is presumed to be a non-Muslim *Munshi* of Samad Khan) states: How can a tyrant win a war? "Yes, wherever a tyrant embarks upon a war, he leaves behind only such people as have been rendered pale with fear." To another question as to how can a tyrant defeat his enemy? "That excepting this that he risks his own neck, he achieves nothing else. Tell him that he will only bite the back of his own hands in shame and grief, because *Deg* and *Teg* were born twins since eternity and they (could not

[24]Karam Singh *Banda Bahadur, op. cit.*, pp. 77-78.

[25]Satish Chandra, *Parties and Politics of Mughal Court,* 1707-1739, p. 68.

be separated). Victory shall never be in store for a tyrant, because victory is the quintessence of such valour as is displayed with the sword of magnanimity and generosity." The author clearly refers to the tyrannous conduct of the Afghans which had resulted in the forfeiture of their right to victory. There were various other causes for the success of Sikhs in that battle. It was their reckless bravery. The unparalleled feats of valour displayed by the hungry, tired, and extremely exhausted Sikhs, whose supplies had run out completely and who were fighting with sore feet, elicited genuine praise from him and he writes that in such straits they left no valour undemonstrated and no feats of courage and audacity unpractised. He writes:

"Lion-like they sprang upon the backs of the elephants, and flung on the ground those who were seated in the *Haudas* (seats on the back of the elephants).

Like leopards (*chitahs*) they would reach such places where even the fastest horse would be reluctant to proceed."

Apart from their personal valour, the Sikhs under Banda had, according to the author, another claim to victory and that was the most important claim. It was Banda's slogan of *Deg* and *Teg* which he had given to the suffering people of the Panjab:

Deg Teg Fateh Nusrat-i-Bedrang
Yaft as Nanak Guru Gobind Singh.[26]

Banda had advocated the victory of *Deg* and *Teg* over oppression and tyranny. He had advocated in his *Hukamnamah* the perpetuation of the Golden Millennium he established with *Deg* and *Teg*. It is crystal clear that the author was deeply influenced by the truthfulness of the right to claim victory for

[26] *Asrar-i-Samadi*, p. 8 (as quoted by Gurbax Singh).

one who wields only the sword of magnanimity and generosity. Though he has condemned in no less categorical terms the excesses committed by Banda, yet he has not been able to deny the truth of the ideal which Banda set before himself and before the entire people of the Panjab, that if victory was to be won, it was to be won only by wielding the sword of generosity. This indirect, but very clear reference to the ideal of the *Deg* and the *Teg* preached by Banda shows the universal popularity Banda and his ideals had achieved in the Panjab.

Ghulam Mohyy-ud-din is the author of *Futuhat Namah-i-Samadi* written in 1722-23 as a biography of Nawab Abdul Samad Khan, who was the governor of Lahore in Banda Bahadur's time. The author calls the Sikh uprising, not a localized affair, but a widespread movement. People all over the hills and plains had risen in revolt and joined Banda Bahadur to expel the Mughals from their land. Once Banda Bahadur had sacked Sirhind and put Wazir Khan to death, he proceeded against the Mughal garrisons in his territory because these were citadels of oppression and imperial strongholds. Mughal garrisons were removed from *thanas* and people from amongst his own followers were put in-charge. The author has stated that the Sikhs made a clean sweep of the aura around the Mughal sovereignty and demolished its majesty altogether. The terror of the Mughal sovereignty had been removed so completely that unmindful of the Mughal might in Panjab, Hindus started pouring into Panjab in large numbers in disguise or even openly by the beat of the drum.

With the *thanas* under their control and the Mughal garrisons expelled and replaced by Sikh garrisons and officials, and the terror of the Mughal sovereignty demolished completely, the Sikhs proceeded to make a more spectacular and more impressive move to declare the emergence of an independent sovereign state in the Punjab. They decided to make a practical move to put a seal on their eastern boundary by declaring the termination of the Mughal sovereignty over the area under their possession. The Sikhs chose the plain of Thanesar to be the scene of their next political rather than military move. They erected a huge giant-sized wooden tower on the other side of the plain of Thaensar touching the western boundary of the Delhi Empire. The practice of setting up of a wooden tower was known to the Indian warriors and they called it a *khamba*. The implication of setting up of such a *khamba* was the assertion of their undisputed right of ownership to the place where the *Khamba* was erected. In Persian history, such a pillar has been called *Satun-i-Jang*. The Sikhs had lofty designs in their minds and they would not be content unless they had become a dominant factor in their own part of the land. They knew that *Thanesar* had a strategic and political importance. All the decisive battles for the mastery over India were fought there. This plain was a scene of the great *Mahabharata* war. The declaration of termination of Mughal sovereignty over Panjab was a step of great daring and momentous political consequences. It was also indicative of the Sikh design to challenge the Mughal Emperor for their right over Panjab.[27]

Ghulam Mohyy-ud-din commends the moral values professed by the Sikhs, though he admits their superiority with a touch of irony. Banda Bahadur had strictly enjoined upon his followers to ban adultery completely from their rank and file.

[27] *Futuhat-Namah-i-Samadi*, pp. 16-20 (as quoted by Gurbax Singh).

Mohyy-ud-din says that they are dirty wretched, unclean and verily devils incarnate, a calamity on earth, descending from the heavens, but they never refer to a woman except as a mother. Mohyy-ud-din, in whose own ranks sexual laxity was the prevalent norm, was surprised at the rigid abstinence of the Sikhs from adultery. He expresses a surprise at such a conduct which appeared abnormal to him. He has therefore said that they never took a woman except for a mother. The Sikhs had adopted a moral code wherein adultery was a heinous crime. Since the Sikhs, according to Banda, were to perpetuate the *Satyug*, i.e. the golden millennium, they were to present themselves as embodiments of moral virtues. Social inequalities born out of caste prejudices had been ruthlessly annihilated, Banda had taken various steps to promote social equality. Not only caste Hindus had joined his ranks in large numbers, the low caste Hindus of Punjab had also volunteered to swell his ranks. These low caste Hindus were termed the dredges of society of the hellish Hindus. Yet these very people after joining the fold of Nanak Parasthan had assumed such formidable strength that the author considered them *afat-i-asmani* i.e. calamity from heavens. When Mughal failed to give them a fight, Mohyy-ud-din justifies their failure on the ground that it is not within the power of a human being to seek confrontation with calamity from heavens.[28]

The *Haqiqat-i-Bina-o-Uruj-i-Firqa-Sikhan* had been written by an anonymous writer in 1784, logically explains the passage of sovereignty from an undeserving authority to a deserving authority, in an *ayat* as under:

[28] *Ibid.*, pp. 20-22, 28, 90-91 (as quoted by Gurbax Singh).

"O Allah! Master of Sovereignty!
Thou givest Sovereignty unto whom Thou wilt.
Thou withdrawest Sovereignty from whom Thou wilt.
Thou abasest whom Thou wilt.
Thou exaltest whom Thou wilt.
In Thy hand is good.
Thou art able to do all things."

The above *ayat* refers to the transfer of sovereignty from Mughals to the Sikhs. Almighty so willed it and, therefore, sovereignty slipped out of the hands of the Mughals. His unconcealed hostility to the Sikhs has however a redeeming feature. It absolves him of any charge of prejudice in favour of the Sikhs. Mughal religious policy, especially their attitude towards the subject people, had witnessed a radical change. These radical measures were reproductive of radical responses and the anti-establishment stance of the Sikhs was the consequent result. Official highhandedness was thus responsible for creating hostility towards the Mughals.[29]

The Guru according to the author sought to uplift the *qaum-i-arazil* i.e. the downtrodden. He was keen on inflicting *khifi* (humiliation) on the *mardum-i-avvan* (the privileged classes). The author shows his awareness of the essentials of Guru's teachings which were aimed at bringing about a new social order by discrediting the old and decrepit feudal structure in which privileges rather than attainments marked the superiority of man. Banda Bahadur's negotiated settlement with Nawab Abdus Samad Khan for the surrender of Garhi at Gurdas Nangal, though honoured in complete and most faithless breach by the

[29] *Haqiqat-i-Bina-o-Uruj-i-Firqa-Sikhan*, p. 3 (as quoted by Gurbax Singh).

Nawab, yet did not fail to underline the Sikh grievances against the Government about which the Sikhs had before surrendering the Garhi secured a definite promise from the Nawab that they would be reported to the Emperor at Delhi.[30]

[30]Gurbax Singh, *Banda's Fall: An Unconditional Surrender or a Negotitated Settlement*, Punjab History Conference proceedings, Vol. VII, p. 59.

III

Sikh Gurus' Wars with the Mughal Forces their Contribution to the Art of Defensive Warfare

With the establishment of Mughal empire, and from the times of Babar till the death of Akbar (1526 A.D. to 1605 A.D.), the Sikh Gurus and their followers were not having any conflict with the ruling Mughal authorities. In fact, Akbar had maintained very cordial relationship with the Sikhs.[1]

Guru Nanak had squarely criticized Babar's invasions and the brutalities and atrocities committed by him and his soldiers on the peaceful population.[2] He had also criticized strongly the Lodhi rulers in not defending their subjects from the invaders.[3] Guru Nanak has even said that a king who cannot protect his subjects is not fit to be a king. Guru Nanak also blamed the subjects even more. According to him, it was the fault of the public which obeyed the orders and showed faithlessness without seeing the right or wrong. He calls such men, who, for the sake of a piece of bread obey like dogs all the orders of the

[1]Gupta Hari Ram, *History of Sikh Gurus*, U.C. Kapoor & Sons, New Delhi. July 1976, p. 93.

[2](i) Tirlochan Singh, *Selections from Sacred Writings of Sikhs*, London, 1960, p. 86.

(ii) *Sri Guru Granth*, Tr Gopal Singh, Gurdas Kapoor & Sons, Delhi. 1960-62, Vol. 1, p. 470.

[3]Macauliffe M.A., *The Sikh Religion*, S. Chand & Co., 1985, Vol. 1, p. 232.

ruler whether right or wrong. He forbade people to obey the orders of an unjust ruler.

Says Nanak, they are human in form, by name,

But in deeds a dog, waiting for the (just or unjust) order at master's door.[4] Guru Nanak held the view that a firm stand has to be taken against misrule. For this the subjects must be prepared for it and not allow the ruler to misuse his authority.[5]

The uniqueness ascribed to Guru Nanak's position lies in the continuity of his work through his successors. The immediate successor of Guru Nanak was also called Nanak and so were all the other successors. The mingling of the light of Guru Nanak with the light of Guru Angad is in accordance with God's raza (will). Guru Gobind Singh is quite emphatic about this unity; in his presentation Guru Nanak becomes Guru Angad and Guru Angad becomes Guru Amar Das and Guru Amar Das becomes Guru Ram Das. Indeed, only the foolish fail to understand that the Gurus were all manifestation of one form and were not distinct from one and another.[6] G.C. Narang writes, "The sword that carved the Khalsa's way to glory was undoubtedly forged by Gobind, but the steel has been provided by Nanak.[7] J.D. Cunningham notes: "It was reserved for Nanak to perceive the true principles of reforms and to lay those broad foundations which enabled his successor Gobind to fire the minds of the country-men with a new nationality and give practical effect to the doctrine that the lowest is equal with the

[4]Kanwarjit Singh, *Political Philosophy of Sikh Gurus*, Atlantic Publishers, Darya Ganj, New Delhi. 1989, p. 108.

[5]*Ibid.*, p. 109.

[6]*Bachittar Natak*, Tr M.L. Peace Jullundhar, undated p. 12.

[7]Narang G.C., *Transformation of Sikhism*, New Book Society, Lahore. 1945, p. 34.

highest. Ernest Trump argues that the disciples of Guru Nanak would, no doubt, have soon dispersed and gradually disappeared as well as the disciples of many other Gurus after Nanak, if he had not taken care to appoint a successor before his death.[8]

J.C. Archer notes that there was something positive and realistic in the reforms of Guru Nanak, something that made a religion and a state.[9] Kapur Singh does not share Arnold Toynbee's views that the order of the Khalsa was a contingent phenomenon dictated by the exigencies of the moment but has been the logical development and entelechy of the teachings of Guru Nanak. Sher Singh writes: Who knows that given the means which Guru Gobind Singh had at his disposal, with the work of ten generations which had prepared the ground for him, Nanak would have met the situation in the same way which the former did in his own time afterwards.[10] Nihar Ranjan Ray observes that to achieve the integration of temporal and spiritual seems to me to have been the most significant contribution of Guru Nanak to the totality of the Indian Way of Life in medieval India.[11]

Guru Angad improved the *lande mahajani,* the language used by Guru Nanak spoken in his verses, in the format of Devnagiri script and named it Gurumukhi script. He reproduced the Bani of Guru Nanak and wrote his own in the Gurumukhi language thereby giving the Sikhs a language of

[8]Trumpp Ernest, *Adhi Granth* (tr), Munshi Ram Manohar Lal, Delhi 1978, p. Lxxvii.

[9]Archer J.C., *The Sikhs,* Princeton USA 1946, p. 60.

[10]Sher Singh, *Philosophy of Sikhism,* Lahore. 1944, p. 24.

[11]Ray Nihar Ranjan, *Sikh Gurus and Sikh Society,* Munshi Ram Manohar Lal, New Delhi. 1975, p. 59.

their own.[12] He also improved the community kitchen called *langar* which was under the personal attention of his wife Mata Khivi.

Guru Amar Das further improved the *langar* and it was made obligatory for all those desirous of meeting the Guru to partake the *langar* food before they could meet him.[13] According to Sikh traditions, even Akbar had to partake the food of the *langar* before meeting the Guru. When Akbar offered some rent free land for the maintenance of the langar the Guru politely declined the offer stating that he had received sufficient resources from his creator.[14] Guru Amar Das made number of practical innovations like emphasis on physical fitness of his disciples, abolished the prevailing practice of *Sati* by widows, he persuaded women not to use *pardha* to cover their faces. He composed the *Anand*, a song of joy to be recited at the time of weddings and other occasions of happiness. Guru Amar Das collected the hymns of Guru Nanak, Guru Angad and his own and put them in the custody of his son, Mohan.

The increasing population of Sikhs all over Punjab was divided into twenty two (22) separate centres of *Sangats* called *Manjis* and put a venerable man in charge of each Manjhi. He also instructed his disciples to visit him along with their family and friends twice a year i.e. on Baisakhi and Diwali.[15] And this practice led to the vast assemblies of Sikh pilgrims on these two occasions at Amritsar. He also abolished most of the useless Hindu customs and ceremonies.

[12]Gupta Hari Ram, *History of Sikh Gurus*, op. cit., p. 82.

[13]Banerjee A.C., *Sikh Gurus and Sikh Religion*, Munshi Ram Manohar Lal, New Delhi. 1983, p. 162

[14]*Ibid.*, p. 165.

[15]Gupta Hari Ram, *History of Sikh Gurus, op. cit.*, pp. 84, 85.

Guru Ram Das shifted to the place which was named Ramdaspura and later on as Amritsar. The Sikhs got a central place as a headquarter of their religion and meeting place on Baisakhi and Diwali festivals.

The fifth Guru Arjan completed the temple in the holy tank of Amritsar. He took up the compilation of the holy book *Adhi Granth* containing the banis of earlier Gurus and a number of saints whose thinking was akin to the thinking of Gurus.[16] The contribution of his Sikhs to the Guru were made uniform, as 10% of their annual income and was called *Daswandh*.

Guru Arjan raised number of buildings. He kept a number of horses and men and lived a very simple life but in the garb of a prince. He was called Sacha Padshah by the Sikhs and with his revenue system of Daswandh he could carry out the construction of Harimandir at Amritsar and other buildings. Abu Fazl writes in the Akbar Nama that the emperor crossed over the Beas at Goindwal and called on Guru Arjan on 24th November, 1598.[17] Sujan Rai Bhandari states that Akbar was very pleased to meet Guru Arjan who greeted him with the recitation of hymns composed by Guru Nanak in praise of God. A state, peaceful and unobtrusive had been slowly evolved, the Guru as its head was called Sacha Padshah of the Panth. The Sikhs had already become accustomed to a form of self-government within the empire.[18]

Jahangir who became emperor in 1605, was already biased against the Sikh Gurus due to his orthodox Islamic leanings. In his autobiography Jehangir writes:

[16]Macauliffe M.A., *The Sikh Religion, op. cit.,* Vol. 3, p. 55.

[17]Gupta Hari Ram, *op. cit.*, p. 93.

[18]Narang G.C., *Transformation of Sikhism, op. cit.*, p. 76.

> "In Goindwal.... There was a Hindu named Arjan, in the garment of sainthood and sanctity, so much so that he had captured many of the simple-hearted Hindus, and even of the ignorant and foolish followers of Islam, by his ways and manners, and they had loudly sounded the drum of his holiness. They called him Guru, and from all sides stupid people crowded to worship and manifest complete faith in him. For three or four generations they had kept this shop warm. Many times it occurred to me to put a stop to this vain affair or to bring him into the assembly of Islam."[19]

Guru Arjan was arrested and taken to Lahore. He was also fined two lakh rupees and was ordered to remove those hymns in the *Granth* which opposed Hinduism and Islam. Jahangir also ordered the Guru to be put to death.[20] Guru Arjan declined the intercession of some Sikhs on his behalf, and prevented his disciples from raising the required amount of fine. Fines, he said, were for thieves, adulterers and slanderers and men devoted to religion never paid fines.[21] Guru Arjan was imprisoned in the Lahore fort. He was tied to a post in the open, exposed to the hot sun of June, burning sand and hot water were thrown on his naked body for five days, plans were to sew him into a raw hide. Guru Arjan sought permission to bathe in the nearby river Ravi. He plunged into the Ravi and never appeared again.[22] Jadu Nath Sarkar in his account of the Sikhs has made some very uncharitable and incorrect remarks. His comment on Guru

[19] *Tuzak-i-Jahangiri* (tr Rodgers and Beveridge), Munshi Ram Manohar Lal, Delhi, 1996 edition, p. 72.

[20] *Ibid.*, pp. 72-73.

[21] Banerjee A.C., *The Sikh Gurus and Sikh Religion, op. cit.*, p. 205.

[22] Gupta H.R., *History of Sikh Gurus, op. cit.*, p. 104.

Arjan that he was a common revenue defaulter and that this collision of the Sikhs with the Mughals in Jahangir's time was entirely due to secular causes have been debated threadbare by later historians and thereafter rejected. Indu Bhushan Bannerjee calls Jadu Nath Sarkar's views "as a perversity of judgment which can hardly be excused in a historian of Sarkar's eminence."[23]

Guru Hargobind became the sixth Nanak, as decided by Guru Arjan, at the age of 11 years. Some historians argue that Guru Hargobind brought about the transformation of the Sikh community from a non-violent religious organization to a military organization.[24] This view is totally incorrect and shows lack of elementary knowledge of the recorded facts of history. The reemergence of orthodox Islamic fanatics after the death of Akbar and under the rule of orthodox Jahangir had been foreseen by Guru Arjan. He arranged for horses and armed retainers.[25] He instructed Baba Budha to train his young son Hargobind in the use of all defensive and offensive weapons, riding, as well as languages, arts and sciences.[26] Shortly before his death, he sent word through his Sikhs that his son Hargobind should sit fully armed on his throne and maintain an army to the best of his abilities.[27] The work of Guru Hargobind was thus, merely a continuation of the work of Guru Arjan and in

[23]Banerjee Indu Bhushan, *Evolution of Khalsa,* Vol. II, p. 6.
[24](i) *Ibid.,* vol. II, p. 8.
(ii) Muhammad Latif, *History of Punjab, op. cit.,* p. 25.
(iii) G.C. Narang, *Transformation of Sikhism, op. cit.,* p. 101.
(iv) Ernest Trumpp, *Adi Granth, op. cit.,* p. Lxxxii.
(v) Macauliffe, *Sikh Religion, op. cit.,* vol. IV, p. 2.
(vi) Cunningham J.D., *A History of Sikhs, op. cit.,* p. 50.
(vii) Gupta Hari Ram, *History of Sikh Gurus, op. cit.,* p. 108.
[25]Gupta Hari Ram, *History of Sikh Gurus, op. cit.,* p. 92.
[26]Macauliffe M.A., *Sikh Religion,* vol. III, p. 50.
[27]*Ibid.,* p. 99.

accordance with the instructions given by Guru Arjan to Baba Budha, the teacher and the guide chosen for Guru Hargobind. Guru Arjan also employed skilled and accomplished warriors to build the nucleus of Guru Hargobind's army. According to Bhai Mani Singh, the concepts of *miri* and *piri* were also introduced by Guru Arjan.

From the very beginning, Guru Arjan had conceived of Sikhism essentially as a state—*Halemi Raj*—the most significant aspect of Sikh sovereignty, by saying that Nanak had founded a state, a dominion of God, a fortress of truth, based on the indestructible foundation of doctrine. Nihar Ranjan Ray has very correctly concluded that Guru Nanak laid the main foundations on which the edifice of Sikh society was to be built. The later Gurus walked on these foundations and a few of them Guru Arjan, Guru Hargobind, and Guru Gobind Singh strengthened them by buttressing and expanding them.[28]

Guru Hargobind at his succession ceremony wore two swords on either side one symbolizing *piri*, the spiritual power and the other *miri*, the temporal power. He stated that in the Guru's house, the spiritual power and the mundane power shall be combined and that his rosary would be the sword belt and that on his turban he would wear the emblem of royalty. He inherited 52 bodyguards, 700 horses, 300 horsemen and 60 gunners.[29] In front of the Harmandir Sahib he built a 12 feet high platform in 1606 called the Akal Takht, God's throne on which he sat in princely attire. The Harmandir was the seat of

[28]Ray Nihar Ranjan, *Sikh Gurus and Sikh Society, op. cit.*, p. 57.

[29]Gupta H.R. *History of Sikh Gurus, op. cit.*, p. 100.

spiritual authority from where he provided the spiritual solace to his disciples, the Akal Takht was the seat of temporal authority from where he dispensed justice like a king in court.[30] This was the position of the Sikh state in the initial making from the inception thereof conceived by Guru Nanak.

Guru Hargobind was imprisoned by Jahangir and kept in the Gwalior fort without specifying any duration. Gwalior fort was reserved for political prisoners of high status. The clear reasons for the arrest and his release later on are not forthcoming, even the actual duration of his imprisonment is not clear. Guru Hargobind's release appears to have been due to the intercession of Mian Mir, a leading sufi saint, who was very friendly with the Sikh Gurus as well as the Mughal royalty.[31] Later on Guru Hargobind had very cordial relationship with the emperor Jahangir, but details of this relationship are not recorded. Guru Hargobind accompanied Jahangir on visit to Kashmir where he met Goswami Ram Dass (Guru of Shiva ji). Goswami asked Guru Hargobind: "I hear you are the successor of Guru Nanak. Guru Nanak had renounced the world, while you wear the sword, keep horses and an army and people call you Sacha Padshah. What kind of a Sadhu are you?" Guru Hargobind replied "Saintliness is within, Sovereignty is without. Baba Nanak had not renounced the world, he had renounced maya." Ram Das was pleased and he later trained Shivaji in the same manner.[32]

Actual hostility between Mughal troops and the Guru broke out in the early years of Shah Jahan's reign, based on rather flimsy

[30]*Ibid.*, p. 110.
[31]Mansukhani Gobind Singh, *Guru Gobind Singh*, 1967, p. 27.
[32]*Ibid.*, p. 28.

grounds. Guru Hargobind decided to defy the Mughal authorities and fought six engagements against the Mughal officials from 1633 to 1638.[33] He kept on shifting his headquarter from Amritsar to Hargobindpur, then to Kartarpur, then to Phagwara, and finally to Kiratpur in the relative safety of the Shivalik range in order to get away from the plains where a major attack by the Mughal forces was quite likely.[34]

Guru Hargobind had fought six battles with imperial troops in a period of five years [1633 to 1638]. A short account thereof is as under:

1. *Battle of Jallo 1633*

Guru Hargobind and Shahjahan were hunting in the same forest, when a quarrel occurred amongst their followers, in which Mughal followers were beaten back by the Sikhs.

2. *Battle of Sangrana 1633*

A large force was sent against the Guru. A battle occurred in Sangrana in which the Mughal force was beaten back.[35]

3. *Battle of Amritsar 1634*

A much larger force was sent to chastise the Guru. After a sharp scuffle Guru shifted to Jhabal, where he performed the nuptial ceremony of his daughter, rather in haste and waited for Mughal army. The pursuing Mughal saw the enormous quantities of sweets and were feasting on the same when Guru gave a surprise

[33]Gupta Hari Ram, *History of Sikh Gurus, op. cit.*, p. 116.
[34]Fani Mohsin, *Dabistan*, p. 235.
[35]Sarkar Jadu Nath, *Short History of Aurangzeb, op. cit.*, p. 156.

attack and defeated the Mughal army, killing many including their commander. Macauliffe writes, "In this battle seven hundred Sikhs defeated an army of seven thousand Mughal troops."[36]

4. *Battle of Lahara 1637*

A disciple of the Guru had gone to Kabul and Balkh to secure some fine horses for the Guru. He collected three fine Arab horses and on his return journey Mohsin Fani was also accompanying him. At Lahore two horses were seized by the governor Khalil Khan. Bidhi Chand, a decoit turned disciple of the Guru, was sent to secure back the horses and he maneuvered to secure back those horses. Khalil Khan sent a large force after the Guru who had moved to Lahara. The Mughal force was repulsed with losses. Mohsin Fani who witnessed all this has squarely blamed Khalil Khan.[37] Jadu Nath Sarkar writes: "Many men came to enlist under the Guru's banner. They said no one else has the power to contend with the emperor."[38]

5. *Battle of Gurusar 1637*

Guru Hargobind was aware of the great power of the Mughal emperor and had temporarily moved into the Lakhi jungle. Kumar Beg and Lal Beg were sent with a large force. The Sikhs lay in ambush and with sudden attack defeated the Mughal force but at a heavy cost of 1200 Sikh soldiers. The scene of the battle was named as Gurusar.[39]

[36]Macauliffe M.A. *Sikh Religion, op. cit.*, Vol. IV, p. 96.
[37]Fani Mohsin, *Dabistan, op. cit.*, p. 239.
[38]Sarkar Jadu Nath, *Short History of Aurangzeb, op. cit.*, p. 156.
[39]Latif Mohamad, *History of Panjab, op. cit.*, p. 256.

6. *Battle of Kartarpur 1638*

A Mughal force was sent under command of Mir Badehra and Paindah Khan against the Guru who had only 5000 men with him. A hard battle was fought in which both the enemy commanders were killed.[40] In this battle Guru's son Tyagmal showed exemplary courage and he was named Teg Bahadur.

Mohsin Fani says that by God's grace Guru had escaped unhurt, though whatever he had has been lost fighting against larger forces. It was impossible for the Guru with his slender resources to maintain a constant struggle against powerful Mughal government.[41] He, therefore, moved into relative safety of the Shivalik hills and set up an establishment named Kiratpur.

Seventh Guru Har Rai (1644-1661) had further moved up in the hills and stayed for 12 years at Nahan.[42] The eighth child Guru Harkrishan (1661-1664) had a very short tenure. The ninth Guru Teg Bahadur (1664 to 1675) had spent time in Patna, Dhaka and Assam and finally came to Makhowal and was arrested and executed under Aurangzeb's orders in 1675.[43]

Guru Gobind Singh, the tenth Guru (1675-1708) became Guru at the age of nine years. He was not destined to have peace in his life-time. He was born in conflict. He was brought up in conflict. He lived in conflict and he died in conflict. This conflict was not of his own making. It was an age of conflict. Conflict was thrust upon him by the force of circumstances, and he had full measure of it. It was a holy conflict. It aimed at

[40]Fani Mohsin, *Dabistan, op. cit.*, p. 235.
[41]*Ibid.*, p. 254.
[42]Gupta Hari Ram, *History of Sikh Gurus, op. cit.*, p. 129.
[43]*Ibid.*, p. 144.

regenerating decaying people and endeavoured to create a new nation, ... says Hari Ram Gupta.[44]

Cordial relations had existed between Gurus and rulers of Sirmaur state since Guru Har Rai times who had lived at Nahan for 12 years. Sirmaur had a boundary dispute with Garhwal who had occupied some of the territory of Sirmaur. Raja of Sirmaur invited Guru Gobind to come to Sirmaur and offered him the site of Paonta on the eastern border with Garhwal on the bank of river Yamuna. His intention was to use Sikhs as his frontier guards against Garhwal.[45] After some reluctance Guru agreed to come to Paonta in 1685. He built a fortress at Paonta.[46] In the peaceful natural beauty, Guru resumed his literary pursuits. He composed *Japu, Akal Ustat, Chandi Charitra, Shastar Nam Mala, Var Sri Bhagwati, Krishan Avtar* etc. Guru had 52 poets in his darbar with whom he used to have the recitations of martial and other literature etc.[47]

Martial activities also received equal attention. Arms, horses, money and men poured in from all sides. Sufi Pir Budhan Shah of Sadhura became his great admirer. On his recommendation Guru employed 500 Pathans settled nearby after release from the Mughal army. The war-like activities of the Sikhs greatly alarmed the hill rajas and they were frightened of the growing power and popularity of the Guru. Guru had established friendly relationship with Ram Rai at Dehra Dun and brought about a somewhat friendly relationship between Sirmaur and Garhwal.[48]

[44] *Ibid.*, p. 148.
[45] *Ibid.*, p. 152.
[46] (i) *Ibid.*, p. 153.
(ii) Santokh Singh, *Suraj Parkash*, p. 2339.
[47] *Ibid.*, p. 153.
[48] Macauliffe M.A., *Sikh Religion, op. cit.*, Vol. V, p. 18.

In a span of 23 years [1682 to 1705], Guru Gobind Singh fought nine battles before the creation of the Khalsa in 1699 and 11 battles after the creation of the Khalsa. A short account thereof is as under:

1. *First Battle of Anandpur 1682*

Bhim Chand Raja of Kahlur was greatly unhappy with the large Sikh gatherings and war-like activities in the vicinity of his capital. Bhim Chand demanded the white elephant and the Persian tent given to the Guru by his devotees. Guru refused it doubting his intentions to retain the same. Bhim Chand led an expedition against Anandpur, but was beaten back with losses.[49]

2. *Second Battle of Anandpur 1685*

Bhim Chand formed alliance with Raja of Kangra and of Guler. They attacked Anandpur in the beginning of the year but were badly beaten back.[50]

3. *Battle of Bhangani, October 1688*

Bhim Chand's son was to get married with the daughter of Raja Fateh Shah of Garhwal. They along with Kirpal Chand of Kangra, Sidh Sain of Mandi and some more hill rajas planned to attack Guru's camp.[51] Medni Prakash of Sirmaur was persuaded to remain neutral.[52] Firstly they seduced away all the 500 Pathans in Guru's employment. Guru sent word thereof to Pir

[49]Giani Kartar Singh, *Kalas Walia*, p. 98-99.
[50]*Ibid.*, p. 503.
[51]Gupta Hari Ram, *op. cit.*, p. 155.
[52]*Ibid.*, p. 155.

Buddhu Shah who immediately sent seven hundred of his men under the command of his four sons to assist the Guru.[53] The enemy force crossed Yamuna a few miles ahead of Paonta. As Guru ji was aware of the entire area, he planned to meet the hill army in the valley of Bhangani and himself occupied a small hillock facing the field of battle which gave him a strategic advantage. Some of his army was kept behind the hillock to be brought into operation at an appropriate time. Heavy casualties occurred on both sides including many leaders. Bhim Chand of Bilaspur and Fateh Chand of Garhwal ran away with their men in the midst of the fight.[54] Battle raged for about eight hours and by sundown enemy troops were nowhere to be seen. With the beat of drum Guru came back to Paonta with his men.

The neutrality of Sirmaur was not liked by Guru ji and he decided to leave Paonta and go back to Anandpur. He raised his camp in November 1688 and sent most of his army to Anandpur and with some troops moved leisurely stopping at Kapal Mochan and Sadhura where he expressed condolences to Pir Buddhu Shah's family. He also stayed at Naraingarh, Raipur Rani. He returned to Anandpur via Ropar and Kiratpur.[55]

4. *Battle of Nadaun, 1690*

Kangra hills were under the charge of Mughal governor at Jammu who sent Alif Khan with a force to subdue some recalcitrant hill rajas. Alif Khan set up his camp at Nadaun on the bank of river Beas. A coalition of hill rajas was made to fight Alif Khan. Guru ji's help was also solicited. Alif Khan was

[53] *Ibid.*, p. 155.
[54] *Ibid.*, p. 155.
[55] Kanhiyalal, *Tarikh-i-Panjab*, Urdu, p. 48-49.

defeated by the hill rajas with the active support of the Guru ji's army; who ran away with his men leaving behind his baggage. Without consulting Guru ji Bhim Chand and Kirpal Singh of Kangra made peace with Alif Khan and agreed to pay tributes to the Mughals which was not liked by Guru ji.

5. *Rustam Khan's Expedition against Anandpur, 1691*

The governor of Lahore was apprised of the increasing strength of the Sikhs who sent a strong force under Rustam Khan to chastise the Guru. Rustam Khan planned a surprise attack on the Sikhs. He camped in the dry bed of a seasonal rivulet opposite Anandpur. Sikhs who used to have an early bath saw the Mughal troops. They immediately reported to the Guru ji and Sikh force was hastily collected and made a forceful attack on the enemy. The Mughal force could not hold against the attack and ran away leaving behind their weapons etc.[56]

6. *The Husaini Battle of Guler, 1693*

Dilawar Khan, governor of Jammu sent another stronger expedition under Hussain Khan in early 1693. In internal expeditions, the general rule was that war must be made to pay for war. Hussain Khan subdued nearby hill rajas and charged levies from them to subdue the Sikhs. Hussain Khan was supported by Kirpal Katoch, Bhim Chand, Himmat Singh, Hari Singh and on the opposite side was Raja Gopal helped by Guru ji and Raja Ram Singh. In the fight Hussain Khan, Kirpal Katoch and Himmat Singh were killed. Guru ji recalls the

[56]Bachhitar Natik, Sec X, Chaupai 1-10.

Husaini Battle in Bachittar Natak as "victory was won and the battle field was left deserted. God Almighty saved us."[57]

7. *Battles of Anandpur, 1694 and 1696*

A newsletter stated: News from Sirhind. Gobind declared himself to be Guru Nanak. Faujdars were ordered to prevent him from assembling Sikhs at Anandpur. A special order was issued to the governor of Sirhind to admonish Gobind, son of Tegh Bahadur. Expeditions were planned in 1694 and 1696 but these failed to achieve any success. No definite details of these battles are available.

9. *Jujhar Singh's Operation, 1697*

Jujhar Singh, a Rajput prince was sent to chastise the Guru. He was assisted by Rustam Khan, representative of governor of Lahore. Gaj Singh of Jaswal was sent by Guru ji with his men, who laid an ambush at Bhalan village and drove away the invading force with heavy casualties. The enemy failed to reach Anandpur.

CREATION OF THE KHALSA, 1699

Mughal forces had suppressed the jat of Tilpat, satnamis of Narnaul, rajputs of Jodhpur and Udaipur, Marathas in the South. The wastage of the Deccan wars which raged intensely for nearly 20 years, was 100000 soldiers and followers and three times that number of horses , elephants, camels, or oxens on the Mughal side every year. Guru Gobind Singh after a most

[57] *Ibid.*, Chaupai 1-10.

determined meditation on the sad state of affairs came to the conclusion that to tyranny was bad, but to bear tyranny patiently was worse. Country did not belong to the King. King belonged to the country and country belonged to the people. If the King was bad people must rise in revolt. Without political liberty, religious, intellectual, social and economic freedom could not be achieved. Political freedom could be won by armies. Armies of the suppressed people were non-existent. For these reasons all the rising against tyranny stated above was suppressed by the Mughal government. Guru Gobind Singh realized that he would have to depend entirely on his own resources. The hill rajputs whom he wanted to use in the national cause had failed. In Krishan Avtar, the Guru says: "No people can have self-rule as a gift from another. It is to be seized through their own strength." With the above view in mind Guru Gobind Singh created the Khalsa. He instituted *khanda pahul* in the place of *charan pahul.* The *pahul* given by Guru ji to the five Sikhs was reciprocated by the five Sikhs by giving the same *pahul* to the Guru. That is how, it is said: "*Waha Guru Gobind Singh, aape Guru te aape chela.* Thus he brought perfect equality among the Sikhs. He totally abolished the outdated caste system. The religious aspect was no less important than the martial aspect. The disciples of Guru Gobind Singh were therefore called saint soldiers. The creation of Khalsa was an epoch-making event in the religious and political history of the country. It marked the beginning of rise of a new people destined to play the role of a hero against all oppression and tyranny. The severities of high caste people over their brethren, the *shudras* were set at naught. As soon as one joins the rank of the Khalsa where all were equal and ready to render one an other every help and useful service.

No people can have self-rule as a gift from another.
It is to be seized through their own strength.[58]

POST KHALSA BATTLES

1. *First Battle of Anandpur, 1699*

The Viceroy of Delhi sent a force of 10000 men under Paindah Khan, Din Beg, some hill chiefs joined them at Ropar. Guru Gobind Singh met them near Anandpur. In the battle, Paindha Khan was killed and Din Begh and hill rajas ran away.[59]

2. *Second Battle of Anandpur, 1699*

Hill rajas under Bhim Chand's leadership and without Mughal assistance sent a message to Guru to leave Anandpur and settle somewhere else. Guru prepared his Sikhs to fight for their survival. The siege lasted for about three months. The Raja Kaiser Chand and Ghamand Chand of Kangra lost their lives. The survivors fled away.[60]

3. *Battle of Nirmohi, 1700*

A strong contingent of Mughal army joined by hill rajas advanced on Anandpur.[61] The Sikh forces intercepted them at Nirmohi, five miles short of Anandpur and drove them away.

[58]Narain Singh, *Guru Gobind Singh,* Chandigarh, 1967, p. 16.
[59]Macauliffe M.A., *Sikh Religion, op. cit.*, Vol. V, p. 124-126.
[60]*Ibid.*, p. 128-37.
[61]Sainapat, *Guru Soba Lahore 1925*, p. 138-42.

4. *Battle of Bharsali, 1700*

Wazir Khan of Sirhind personally assumed the command and attacked Anandpur. The Sikhs suffered defeat and retreated towards Bharsali about 40 kms away from Anandpur. The invaders pursued the Sikhs and another engagement took place at Bharsali. After some time, the invading force left for Sirhind and Sikhs again occupied Anandpur.

5. *Third Battle of Anandpur, 1702*

Mughal commander Sayyad Beg and Alif Khan were going back to Delhi. Bhim Chand to persuaded them to help him expel the Sikhs from Anandpur on payment of Rs. 1000 per day. After a couple of skirmishes differences arose in the invading parties and they left the area.[62]

6. *Fourth Battle of Anandpur, 1703*

Bhim Chand again made an alliance of few hill rajas and marched on Anandpur. Sikhs met them outside the town and a tough battle was fought. Hill rajas fell back and dispersed.

7. *Fifth Battle of Anandpur, 1703*

Bhim Chand again sought help of Mughal Viceroy at Delhi. A strong force was dispatched and Guru ji came to know of it when they had reached Thanesar. The defence of Anandpur was organized. Sayyad Beg and Maiman Khan stood with the Guru. The enemy forces were able to drive Sikhs out of Anandpur and plundered the town. The Sikhs returned back when the heavily

[62]Macauliffe M.A., *Sikh Religion, op. cit.*, Vol. V, p. 153-54.

laden enemy troops were moving out. A fierce battle was fought and the Sikhs recovered back Anandpur.[63]

The institution of *masands* had got corrupted over the passage of time and was abolished by Guru Gobind Singh. The notorious *masands* were severely punished. Others had to pay fines.[64]

8. *The Sixth and Last Battle of Anandpur, 1704*

Anandpur was closely besieged in Sept 1704 by Mughal forces from Delhi, Sirhind, Lahore and Jammu and Hindu hill rajas of Kuler, Kangra and others. Wazir Khan, faujdar of Sirhind assumed the command of entire force.[65] Sikhs had mounted two guns on the fort and they took a heavy toll of the enemy troops. Wazir Khan lost 900 men on the first day.[66]

All the routes of ingress and egress were cut off. Besides acute shortage of food, supplies of war material were also getting exhausted. There occurred certain desertions also. Wazir Khan and hill rajas gave promise of safe passage in case the Guru leaves Anandpur.[67]

Under pressure from inside people and outside enemies, Guru ji decided to leave Anandpur on 20-21 December, 1704.[68] Wazir Khan attacked the Guru's camp. There were lot of casualties on the Guru's side both on account of the enemy attack and the swollen rivulet. Guru's party of 400 men was left of only

[63] *Ibid.*, p. 156, 162-64.
[64] Bachhittar Natik, Sec XII, Chaupai 10.
[65] Gupta Hari Ram, *History of Sikh Gurus, op. cit.*, p. 202.
[66] *Ibid.*, p. 203.
[67] Santokh Singh, *Sri Guru Partap Suraj Granth*, p. 5819-22.
[68] Gupta Hari Ram, *History of Sikh Gurus, op. cit.*, p. 205.

43 persons. Guru's family was also split. Guru was in a very delicate position with Mughal forces both in front and at the back and hill rajas on the left pursuing them like wild dogs. Guru turned to the right, reached Chamkaur where he occupied a mud-built double storeyed house with a large compound.[69] By next morning the house was besieged by 700 cavalry with artillery. An envoy was sent to the Guru asking him to surrender and negotiations for the same started. By evening only 5 Sikhs were left with the Guru. His two elder sons had also died fighting. The five Sikhs met in a conclave and took the decision that Guru should escape. The five Sikhs thereafter announced the decision to the Guru and Guru accepted the same with reluctance.[70]

GURU ESCAPES TOWARDS MALWA DESERT

Guru ji and three companions reached Macchiwara in the morning. Ghani Khan and Nabhi Khan helped Guru in escaping and he reached Dina. At Dina he got the news that his younger sons and mother were betrayed by their cook and delivered to Wazir Khan. On refusal of the young ones to embrace Islam, they were bricked alive and executed. Their grandmother died of shock. His wives could not reach Nahan but had reached Delhi in disguise of Jat woman.[71]

While at Kot Kapura Guru received news that Sirhindi troops were following him. Guru chose a place named Khidran with a water pound at the start of desert area. Here he celebrated Baisakhi on 29th March 1705 with his Sikhs.

The forty Sikhs who had left Guru at Anandpur were persuaded by a lady Bhago and they joined back with the Guru.

[69] *Ibid.*, p. 207.
[70] *Ibid.*, p. 209.
[71] *Ibid.*, p. 211.

The enemy after sustaining heavy losses retired towards Sirhind.[72] Mai Bhago followed the Guru ji and died at Nander.

PRINCIPLES TO BE OBSERVED IN WAR

War is considered as one of the methods of settling disputes among the belligerent parties or states. The war is a contest carried on by public force between states or between states and communities. Laws of war existed in some form or the other with the establishment of organized society and states. In Greece there was a religious body called Amphictyonic Council.[73] This Council used to arbitrate over the disputes amongst the city states to avoid war and in case of war to mitigate its horrors by suggesting ways and means for it, violation of which was forbidden. During the ascendancy of Rome, a Fetial law was passed which made obligatory that a demand for satisfaction from the enemy be made before the initiation of war.[74] The prisoners of war were to be treated with compassion. In India, Manu Smriti has suggested such laws viz. not to use concealed weapons, arrows smeared with poison; enemy who had surrendered or fled away was not to be killed; disarmed or sleeping persons were not to be harmed; wounded were not to be attacked, etc. In Mahabharata, Bhisma advised Yudhisthira not to conquer any territory by unrighteous means, even if subjugation of such territories by unrighteous means makes him a sovereign of the whole earth. Woman of the invaded area must not be attacked and area should not be plundered.

[72] *Ibid.*, p. 219, 220.

[73] Kanwarjit Singh, *Political Philosophy of Sikh Gurus*, Atlantic Publishers, New Delhi, 1989, p. 112.

[74] *Ibid.*, p. 112.

In spite of all the above measures brutalities of war could not be stopped for the reasons that these laws were rarely put into practice and there was no authority strong enough to enforce such laws. What little sanctity existed with regard to such laws in India simply vanished with the advent of Islamic invaders for whom carrying out brutalities, large-scale slaughter of men, enslavement of women and children was the normal practice.[75]

The Sikh Gurus Guru Hargobind and Guru Gobind Singh who maintained armies and fought battles with the Mughal forces and Hindu hill rajas, had fought all the battles for defensive purposes and not with the purpose of acquiring new territories. These wars were only for the protection of their faith and their disciples. They have laid down certain rules of fighting such battles to save themselves from oppression. The rules laid down by the Sikh Gurus were not only followed by themselves, they preached the Sikhs to follow the same. Guru Nanak has said that one should attack only that person or party who has at least equal strength to that of the invader. One should not attack the weaker. "If the powerful duel with the powerful, I grieve not; But if a ravenous lion falls upon a flock of sheep, then the Master must answer."[76] Sikh Gurus have laid great emphasis on peace and have permitted war only as a last resort.

"When all efforts to restore peace,
Prove useless and no words avail
Lawful is the flash of steel then
And right it is the sword to hail. – Guru Gobind Singh[77]

[75] *Ibid.*, p. 114.
[76] *Adi Granth*, p. 360.
[77] Guru Gobind Singh, *Bachhittar Natik*, V. 22.

Nearly all wars, in history, have been fought for money, woman and territories. Guru Hargobind and Guru Gobind Singh fought many wars but they did not make any personal gain out of them. They fought against tyranny and to defend the rights of human beings. The following laws seem to have been practiced by Sikh Gurus.

1. *Not to attack unarmed or the weak*

When Guru Hargobind attacked Painde Khan, the latter's horse was killed. In keeping with the ethics of war the Guru also dismounted himself to fight at equal level. Kavi Sohan depicts the situation in the Gurbilas Patshahi-6:

> The Guru aimed and gave a blow with the left hand
> Painde Khan fell on the ground and began to cry
> Guru left his horse and came on foot and challenged him.[78]

Guru Gobind Singh has given an account of battle of Bhangani in Bachittar Natak. Guru ji when came face to face with Harichand of Hindur, he gave him a fair chance to fight. Hirachand's first arrow killed Guru's horse. The second arrow grazed Guru's ear and the third penetrated the buckle of Guru's waistbelt and just pricked his body. Thereafter Guru took aim at Harichand and struck him with an arrow. He died instantaneously and his soldiers ran away.[79]

2. *To challenge before attack*

Even in a war first a prior challenge should be given to the other party and if the other party does not submit to the challenge,

[78]Gurbilas Patshahi-6, 20.575-76.
[79]Guru Gobind Singh, *Bachhittar Natik*, viii, 34.

then alone, an attack can be resorted to. Enemy is not to be taken unaware of and not to be attacked from the back. Banda Bahadur also used to issue parwanas and send through a messenger and on refusal of the opposing party to submit, he used to attack.[80]

In the Zafarnama, Guru Gobind Singh condemned the act of Mughal army which attacked the Guru without any challenge.

> What more forty famished men can do
> In a bloody combat of hellish hue
> When a million armed foes pounce
> Unawares upon them in moments few.[81]

3. *Not to plunder private property or the property of peaceful citizens*

Sikh Gurus have all along enjoined on their soldiers not to plunder private property or property of private citizens. When the commander of Lahore army, plundered the Doon area, he looted the property of peaceful citizens even. Guru Gobind Singh has condemned the same in Bachittar Natak.

> He plundered the Doon and none could challenge him
> He divided the booty amongst his men and thus he did this nefarious act.

4. *Treatment to be accorded to Ladies and Children*

In Sikhism women are given a place of honour. Bhai Gurdas says:

> When we see other men's wives beautiful we should consider them as our mothers, sisters and daughters.

[80] Ganda Singh, *Banda Bahadur, op. cit.*, p. 154.
[81] *Guru Gobind Singh, Zafarnama,* V. 19.

To covet another's women is forbidden to a Sikh as the Swine is to the Muslim and the cow to the Hindu.[82]
The Sikhs told the Guru that Muslim soldiers raped the Hindu women
Why not the Sikhs take revenge? Why does the Holy Granth forbid this?
The Guru assured, 'I've to take you much higher
I don't want you to go downwards, that is why
I forbid to commit sins.[83]

Qazi Nur Muhammad who accompanied Ahmad Shah Abdali wrote that Sikhs never touched a Muslim woman who came in their way, called her mother and took her out of the fighting zone.

5. *To help the opposing party for the cause of Righteousness*

This is a unique convention set by Guru Gobind Singh to help even the enemy for the cause of righteousness. The Sikh Gurus fought only for the sake of righteousness. Though Guru Gobind Singh fought the battle of Bhangani against the hill chiefs led by Bhim Chand yet he had no hesitation in making a common cause with those very hill chiefs when the latter were attacked by the Mughal force. The joint armies of the hill chiefs and of the Guru repelled the attack in the battle of Nadaun.[84] Guru Gobind Singh has given the description of the battle in 11th Chapter of the Bachitra Natak.

[82]Bhai Gurdas, Var 6.8.
[83]Santokh Singh, *Gur Parkash Suraj Granth*, 6.20, 16-19.
[84]Bachittar Natak, Chapter XI.

6. *No violation of Treaty/Agreement*

According to the Sikh thought, once one has made some commitment, he should not run away from his words. This is to be applied during wars as well. If a party makes some promise or agreement, it should sincerely honour them. When Aurangzeb promised Guru Gobind Singh that he would not attack the Guru if the latter vacated the fort of Anandpur. The emperor went back from his promise and his forces attacked the Guru when he left Anandpur Sahib on his promise. Guru Gobind Singh has criticized the same in the Zafarnama addressed to the emperor.

Keep in view thy solemn oaths O King,
And abide by them to thy level best
Stick to the positions once taken up
Within and without the same be you
Had I (Guru) even in secret taken oath
On the holy Book as didst thou
I would never take a single step
Beyond the mark set by that vow.[85]

7. *No General Massacre*

In medieval period, Muslim invaders killed the general public in mass massacres. The Indian history is replete with numerous examples in which thousands of Indians were butchered by the invading Islamic forces right from Mohammad Bin Qasim to the end of Mughal dynasty. In Zafarnama Guru Gobind Singh asked Aurangzeb not to commit cruelties on the humble and the

[85] *Guru Gobind Singh, Zafarnama,* V. 53, 55, 18.

low general public who had not committed any sin against the emperor.

When with thy cruel hand O Alamgir
You do torment the humble and low
You slash your own oaths one by one
With the dagger sharp blow by blow.[86]

8. *Not to damage the places of Worship*

The history of Islamic rule in India is full of instances of killing of Hindus, demolishing of their temples and erecting mosques in their place. This was because the Muslims took the Hindus as infidels and treated them as their slaves. Bhai Gurdas condemned demolishing of temples in his first Var while depicting the situation on the eve of Guru Nanak's birth.

The temples are razed to the ground,
And mosques are erected in their place
The sin is prevailing
The temple and the mosque are the same.
The Hindu worship and the Muslim prayer are the same;
All men are the same;
It is through error they appear different.[87]

9. *Not to harm persons who have surrendered*

The Sikh Gurus laid down the rule that whosoever surrenders must be protected because our Lord also does so:

[86] *Ibid.*, V. 106.
[87] *Guru Gobind Singh*, Akal Ustati 16/86.

Whoever seeks Lord's Refuge, him He hugs to His bosom:
This is the innate nature of the Lord.[88]

Similarly the third Guru, Amardas, says:

And he who seeks Thy Refuge, him Thou Redeemest.

But this rule was never obeyed by the Islamic forces and the execution of Banda Bahadur with torture along with his followers in 1716 by the Mughal emperor is the height of brutality and inhumanism.[89]

10. *Treatment of the Injured after the battle*

Some of the disciples complained to Guru that a Sikh called Kanhaya had been giving water and aid not only to the wounded Sikhs but also to the wounded enemies. Guru asked Kanahya if this was true. "Yes, my Lord, it is true in a sense," said Kanahya "I have been giving water to every one who needed it on the field of battle, but I saw no Mughals or Sikhs there. I saw only the Guru's face every where." The Guru was pleased with his reply, blessed him and told his Sikhs that Kanahya had understood his teachings correctly.[90] Thus, started the Red Cross of the Sikhs at the battle front.

[88] *Sri Guru Granth*, p. 544.
[89] Ganda Singh, *Banda Bahadur, op. cit.*, p. 234.
[90] Harbans Singh, *Heritage of the Sikhs*, Manohar, 1994, p. 89.

IV

Battle Strategy of Banda Bahadur

Banda Bahadur with meager resources in men and materials, i.e. requisite number of trained soldiers, arms, ammunition and food supplies, fought numerous battles against Mughal forces having much larger and trained armies with unending supply lines of soldiers, arms, ammunition and food-stocks etc. In spite of these disparities, Banda Bahadur won many battles. Sikh Gurus had breathed an undying spirit of sacrifice in the Sikh volunteers. These soldiers fighting and dying for the faith had a greater edge over those who were fighting for the sake of wages only. Banda Bahadur added his battle strategies to the valour of Sikh volunteers which resulted in the victories of the Khalsa.

With the coming of the Muslim rulers in India, a large number of Muslim camp followers also came to India and were looting and harassing the common public. To counter them the Hindu *deras* and *maths* who were having ascetic warriors for their protection greatly increased their strength. Hindu ascetic warriors used certain military strategies which were very essential when their numbers were lesser than the armies against whom they had to fight.

The guerilla style of rapid attack-retreat-reattack had been used by them since ages. They also used the surprise element and would make lightning attacks on their opponents especially in dark hours.

Banda Bahadur also made extensive use of these strategies. It was the combined effect of the spirit of sacrifice in the men and war strategies of Banda Bahadur that made Sikhs win wars against much larger Mughal forces.

These battle strategies had been used by the ascetic warriors of India, after them by Banda Bahadur and thereafter by the Sikh Misls in their fight with the Mughals and Afghans. It was called '*dhai path*' i.e. two and a half steps.

There are about 30 books which give account of various battles fought by Banda Bahadur with the Mughal forces. Of all the accounts by various authors, the chronological account of the battles of Banda Bahadur and the detailed description of facts regarding each battle are well portrayed by Ganda Singh in his book *Life of Banda Singh Bahadur*. Therefore, the descriptional details of various battles have been taken from the above-said work of Ganda Singh whereas stress has been mainly on the strategical appreciation of these battles. Almost every battle won by Banda Bahadur had a distinct contribution of the strategies employed by him.

The strategy portion of the battle accounts is given in **bold** print for the convenience of the readers to locate the same.

1. Bangar (Hissar) to Sirhind

Banda Bahadur, on becoming a disciple of Guru Gobind Singh, moved to Guru's camp.[1] He was given an insight on the situation in Punjab vis-à-vis the Sikhs and the Mughals, and presumably some instructions deemed necessary by Guru Gobind Singh to be followed by Banda as and when situations so developed. The

[1]Gupta Hari Ram, *History of the Sikhs*, Vol. II, 1978, page 7.

THE SIKH UNDER BANDA BAHADUR 1709-1715

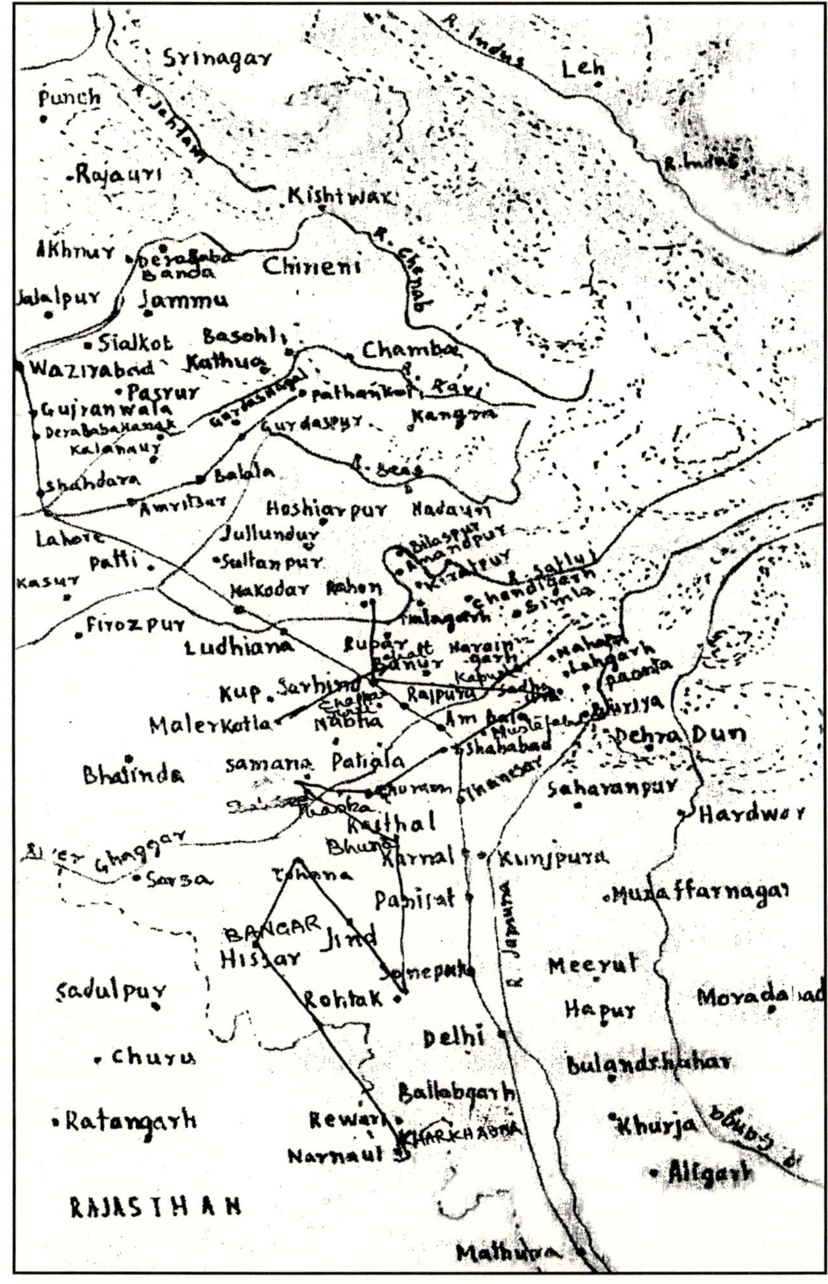

directions given by Guru ji to Banda Bahadur were only between them and there was no body else privy thereto. Historians have given all sorts of varying accounts as to what directions were given by Guru ji to Banda Bahadur. Since there is no contemporary record or even oral evidence of any body privy to the instructions, the entire varying accounts are fictional fabrications of the various historians and cannot be credited with any historical authenticity.[2] Banda was given five advisors, senior Sikhs with Guru Gobind Singh and about 20 soldiers. Shortly after Banda Bahadur left for Panjab in October 1708, he got the news of the sad demise of Guru Gobind Singh at the hands of a fanatic assassin from Sirhind.[3] Banda took extreme precautions to avoid contact with the Mughal espionage network and a distance of about 1600 kms was covered in a year's time, which ordinarily could have been covered in about three months. He took circuitous routes and reached the town of Kharkhauda about 30 kms short of Delhi, the Mughal capital.[4]

Banda Bahadur tried to settle down and study the various aspects of the situation regarding his resolve to teach a lesson to the rulers of Sirhind who had executed the two younger sons aged 9 and 7 of Guru Gobind Singh. He became popular with

[2]Ganda Singh, *Banda Singh Bahadur*, Amritsar, 1935, p. 25.

[3]Gupta Hari Ram, *op. cit.*, p. 6.

[4]*Ibid.*, p. 7.

"Banda seems to have travelled in disguise and by circuitous routes to avoid detection. Generally he adopted the same route across Maharashtra and Rajasthan as was followed by Guru Gobind Singh. The distance between Nander and Hissar in Haryana by that route was 1,600 kms. At the rate of 16 kms or 10 miles a day on an average, Banda should not have taken more than 100 days during his journey, but he actually took about a year. It means that he might have been frequently in hiding. The Mughal spy system was most elaborate during Aurangzeb's period. Had Banda and his party come to their notice, it would have been eliminated. That is why Banda travelled right across Maharashtra and Rajasthan, both of which were in revolt against the Mughals."

the people by giving blessings of "Dudh Put" (Milk and Son) to the locals who would seek his blessings.[5] He found that professional gangs of dacoits were in the habit of raiding and looting nearby prosperous villages of Banghar area (Hissar). These dacoits at times used to give the warning of their attack and rich people would generally leave their houses at the mercy of dacoits.[6]

On one such occasion, Banda Bahadur encouraged the 'panches' of the village to stay back and face the dacoits, but the city fathers were not prepared to accept his advice. Banda Bahadur locked them up in a house on the night of the attack.[7]

Banda Bahadur had found out that the dacoits collected in a close-by mangrove and from there attacked the village after allotting positions to the various members of the gang. Before the arrival of the dacoits, Banda Bahadur put his men on the tree tops, at the place dacoits used to assemble. The instructions to men were to jump down on the dacoits just when they were prepared to attack the village. Banda Bahadur's attack was so sudden and bold that the dacoits were thrown into confusion, their leader was captured and those who had come to rescue him were also captured or killed.[8] Banda Bahadur released the 'panches' and ordered the pursuit of the robbers who were chased to their very homes.[9]

Banda Bahadur thus gained the sympathy and confidence of the villagers. He now publicly proclaimed that he would

[5]Ganda Singh, *Banda Singh Bahadur, op. cit.*, p. 27.
[6]*Ibid.*, p. 29.
[7]*Ibid.*, p. 29.
[8]*Ibid.*, p. 29.
[9]*Ibid.*, p. 30.

undertake to protect the poor and the helpless against all professional robbers and official tyrants and for that he expected no reward from the people in lieu of the service rendered except some simple necessities of rations, milk and curd etc.[10] He further invited people in the fold of the Khalsa brotherhood and promised them a share in the booty and the conquered land.[11]

Banda Bahadur now dispatched the Guru ji's letters to the Sikhs in Malwa, Doaba and the Majha districts of Panjab calling upon them to join him in the laudable object of uprooting the tyrannous rule of the intolerant Mughals.[12] His companions from Nanded as well, wrote large number of letters to the leading Sikhs all over the country telling them that Banda Bahadur had been appointed by Guru ji himself as Jathedar of the Khalsa and that every true Sikh to join under his banner.[13]

The first town to be attacked was Sonepat by a small force of about 500 Sikhs. The faujdar of Sonepat was a careless fellow who came ill-prepared to oppose the advancing Sikhs so as he was soon routed and made to flee the field.[14]

Banda Bahadur received the information that a small military detachment escorting a treasure of revenue collections from a number of districts was halting at the village Bhuna, on their way to Delhi. Banda Bahadur with his followers immediately reached the village and finished the Mughal force guarding the treasure and took possession thereof without any opposition.[15] The raid of Banda Bahadur on the imperial

[10] *Ibid.*, p. 30.

[11] *Ibid.*, p. 30.

[12] *Ibid.*, p. 31.

[13] *Ibid.*, p. 31.

[14] Gupta Hari Ram, *op. cit.*, pp. 9-10.

[15] Deol G.S., *Banda Bahadur*, New Academic Publishing Co., Jullandhar, 1972, p. 33.

treasury was reported to the *Amil* of Kaithal, a Hindu commander, who at once hurried to the site with the troops of his cavalry. Banda Singh and his men hid themselves behind some old walls, trees etc. When they found that the enemy could be successfully surprised, they rushed out of the hiding places, leapt at their horses and threw many of them off their saddles. The *Amil* was captured. He was, however, released on the condition of handing over all his horses to the Sikhs to which he readily agreed.[16] He was allowed to retain his office on behalf of the Khalsa on payment of requisite tribute and a detachment of Sikh soldiers was detailed with him for collection of revenue.[17] The Amil of Kaithal to pay tribute and a Khalsa detachment to help collection of revenue, was the first administrative measure in setting up of the Sikh State.

Banda Bahadur who was running short of funds distributed liberally the entire booty amongst his followers.[18] Sikhs were now preparing to attack Samana. This was a town in occupation of a number of 'Sayyads' and 'Mughal *Zamindars*'. Jalal-ud-din, the executioner of Guru Tegh Bahadur and Shashal Begh and Bashal Begh, the executioners of young sons of Guru Gobind Singh were also residents of Samana.[19]

The town of Samana was very well fortified with a strong wall and every haveli (large house) was a fortress by itself. On the morning of 26th November, 1709, Banda Bahadur and his men suddenly rushed into the town from a distance of a few miles and entered it from all sides before the gates could be

[16]Ganda Singh, *op. cit.*, p. 36.

[17]*Ibid.*, p. 37.

[18]Gokul Chand Narang, *Transformation of Sikhism*, New Book Society, Lahore, 1945

[19]Deol G.S., *op. cit.*, p. 35.

closed against them.[20] This strategy gave lot of dividends in the form of saving many Sikhs' lives, which could have been lost had the gates been closed before the attack. In the attack of the Sikhs on the havelis, the desperate and infuriated peasants of the neighbouring villages also joined the Sikhs to wreak their vengeance on the hated Mughals and set their houses on fire. Before nightfall, the beautiful town of Samana, with its lofty buildings was converted into a heap of ruins never to regain its past glory.[21] About 10,000 lives are said to have been lost, majority of them being Mughals.

Banda Bahadur greatly impressed by the bravery of Bhai Fateh Singh appointed him the Faujdar of Samana. Samana has generally been called by historians as the first regular conquest of Banda Bahadur.[22] Wazir Khan of Sirhind was greatly alarmed at the Sikh invasions and had sent some spies to Samana to gather information. These spies were caught and brought before Banda Bahadur. He ordered them to be given a good shoe-beating and then sent back to Wazir Khan.[23]

The contemporary historian Khafi Khan has written: "In two or three months' time, four to five thousand pony-riders, and seven to eight thousand warlike footmen joined Banda Bahadur. Day by day their number increased, and abundant money and material by pillage fell into their hands. Soon eighteen to nineteen thousand men in arms under him raised

[20]Ganda Singh, *op. cit.*, p. 39.

[21]Ganda Singh, *op. cit.*, p. 40. Thus, before nightfall, the beautiful town of Samana, with its palatial buildings, was converted into a heap of ruins, never to regain its past glory.

[22]*Ibid.*, p. 41.

[23]*Ibid.*, pp. 41-42.

aloft the standard of plunder and persecution."[24] Further on he says: "Numerous villages were laid waste, and he appointed his own police officers (*thanedars*) and collectors of revenue (*tahsildar-e-mal*).[25]

Next came the town of Ghuram, which was plundered and put under the charge of Bhai Fateh Singh, the Faujdar of Samana.[26] Thaska surrendered without offering any resistance.[27] The next towns were Thanesar and Shahbad inhabited by the Mughal Sayyads and Shaikhs, but none dared to oppose the Sikhs. Then, the town of Mustafabad came in the way of Sikh troops.

The local Faujdar had 2,000 imperial troops and two large guns. On the appearance of artillery, many of the gangs of plunderers who had started following Banda Bahadur for the prospects of booty deserted him. Banda Bahadur encouraged and rallied his brave Sikhs and made so desperate an attack that the Mohammadan soldiers fled leaving their canons behind them.[28] After this victory, several of the deserters returned and joined Banda Bahadur's army.

Banda Bahadur was now moving towards the next biggest town of Sadhaura and the town of Kapuri which was ruled by Qadam-ud-din. There was hardly a pretty Hindu woman whose chastity had not been attacked by this depraved ruler by his force of arms.[29] His woman hunting expedition was not confined to his territories, he is said to have forcibly carried away a Sikh

[24]Khafi Khan, *Muntakhab-ul-Lubab*, quoted by Gupta Hari Ram, *op. cit.*, p. 10
[25]Gupta Hari Ram, *op. cit.*, p. 10.
[26]Deol G.S., *op. cit.*, p. 36.
[27]*Ibid.*, p. 36.
[28]*Ibid.*, p. 37.
[29]Ganda Singh, *op. cit.*, p. 45.

woman from the city of Amritsar entering her house in the disguise of a Sikh.[30]

The passions of the Sikh volunteer force having been greatly aroused by the misdeeds of Qadam-ud-din, they fell upon Kapuri, overpowered the resistance offered by its residents and set on fire the strongholds of Qadam-ud-din. He is said to have perished in the general conflagration.[31]

Banda Bahadur's next expedition was against Sadhura. Its ruler Usman Khan was notorious for the oppression of his subjects.[32] He was the same man who had tortured to death the great Muslim saint Sayyad Badr-ud-din Shah, popularly known as Sayyad Budhu Shah, whose family members and followers were also given the same fate and none was allowed to be buried and all were burnt, simply because he had helped Guru Gobind Singh in the battle of Bhangani against the Hindu hill rajas.[33] Hindus were subjected to every kind of indignity, even their dead were not allowed to be burnt.[34] Sadhura is a corrupted form of Sadhu-wara, or the abode of Sadhus which in the days of Buddhist ascendancy was one of their holy places.[35] Macauliffe has stated that Sikh forces fought with great bravery, captured the fort and leveled it to the ground. This does not seem to be correct position. Macauliffe has stated that "Banda Bahadur attacked Sadhura fort and the Imperial forces stationed there came forth to oppose them but were easily defeated. They fled and took shelter behind the city walls. Banda Bahadur's forces

[30] *Ibid.*, p. 45.
[31] *Ibid.*, p. 46.
[32] *Ibid.*, p. 46.
[33] *Ibid.*, p. 47.
[34] *Ibid.*, p. 47.
[35] *Ibid.*, p. 47.

with great bravery captured the fort and leveled it to the ground."[36] Had there been a fort he would have used it rather than wasting his time and energy in destroying it. The statement of Macauliffe seems to be incorrect. Ganda Singh, Sohan Singh, M.S. Ahluwalia, H.R. Gupta, Gokul Chand Narang and H.K. Sagoo have not mentioned the existence of any fort at Sadhura while writing about the attack and occupation of Sadhura by the Sikhs. M.S. Chandla quotes Sukhdial Singh that "the haveli of Pir Budhu Shah had become '*Qatal Garhi*'. The fort and the haveli were reduced to smoking rubble and the animals like horses and camels were captured by the Singhs" in support of the Macauliffe's statement. The town of the Sadhura has been examined on number of occasions. What seems to be the ground position is that there may have been a wall around the town for general security purposes, but no fort existed as no foundation etc. thereof are visible.

After occupation of the Sadhura town, Banda Bahadur seems to have made some entrenchments close to the town for use of his troops from where the Sikhs fought the Mughal army in 1710 and 1711.

With the advance of Banda Bahadur's army on Sadhura, the peasants all around who had been bullied and harassed by Usman Khan and his officials got an opportunity to have a revenge against them and they joined Banda Bahadur in great number to loot and destroy the properties of the rich Sayyads and Sheikhs. Bloody battles ensued between the masses and the Sayyads and Sheikhs to an extent that it was not possible for

[36]Macauliffe M.A., *The Sikh Religion,* S. Chand & Co., New Delhi (First published in 1909), p. 247.

Banda Bahadur and his soldiers to stop the same.[37] They also located the rich Sayyads and Sheikhs who had hidden themselves in the haveli of Shah Badr-ud-din believing it to be a safe place, and put them to death. The haveli to this day is called '*Qatal Garhi'* or the slaughter house.[38]

Another story goes that couple of Sikhs were having difficulty in taming their camel. They saw a fellow going with a strong 'lathi', took his 'lathi' and gave few blows to the camel. The lathi broke down and lot of letters fell out of it. These letters were written by all the important Muslim residents to Wazir Khan to come and attack Sikhs and save them from disgrace and indignity.[39]

Banda Bahadur called a meeting of all the prominent Muslim leaders, showed them these letters, which made each one begging for mercy. Banda Bahadur is said to have told them to get into one house which they consider safe, but certain punishment had to be awarded to the town. All the rich Muslims went into the haveli of Badr-ud-din, which has an enclosed area of about an acre or so. Banda Bahadur let his Singhs to kill all the people assembled in the haveli and hence the place was called 'Qatal Garhi'.

The building has been taken over by a Jain organization which demolished the same step by step to build a school. The outer gate and walls all around alone are standing till date. Both Sukhdyal Singh and M.S. Chandla are wrong in stating that Sikhs burnt down the Haveli of Pir Budhu Shah.[40] These sites

[37]Ganda Singh, *op. cit.*, p. 49.

[38]*Ibid.*, p. 49.

[39]Sohan Singh, *Life and Exploits of Banda Singh Bahadur*, Punjabi University, Patiala (First published in 1915), pp. 45-46.

[40]Chandla M.S., *Bahadur*, Aurva Publications, Chandigarh, 2006, p. 122.

being close-by have lately been examined and correct position stated. The allegation that Sikhs destroyed the old Mausoleums and burnt the dead bodies is totally incorrect as the Mausoleums of Ganj-i-Ilam and Qutab-ul-Aqtab stand intact to the present day in the same condition in which these were before Banda Bahadur's invasion.[41]

The Hindus of Chhat complained to Banda Bahadur that they were being greatly harassed by the Muslim rulers. Banda Bahadur sent a detachment which occupied the small town of Chhat and a Sikh Amil was posted there.[42] Chhat is close to Banur. Banda was waiting for the Sikh troops from Majha to join him before he takes the final plunge with Wazir Khan, faujdar of Sirhind. Sikhs had crossed Sutlej and reached Kiratpur.

Large number of Sikhs from Doaba and Majha were soon expected to join Banda Singh.[43] Wazir Khan was greatly worried and he was devising ways and means of preventing the combination of the two forces. He sent Sher Mohammad Khan of Maler Kotla along with his brother and cousins with various other resources of warfare to go and stop the Sikhs at Ropar.[44] Majha troops who had reached Ropar were attacked by Sher Mohammad Khan with much greater force than that available with the Sikhs. The battle was going in favour of Pathans due to their better fire power. Sikh commanders decided to keep their soldiers in the trenches to save them from artillery fire.[45]

[41]Ganda Singh, *op. cit.*, p. 49.
[42]Deol G.S., *op. cit.*, p. 39.
[43]*Ibid.*, p. 41.
[44]*Ibid.*, p. 41.
[45]*Ibid.*, p. 41.

As the day was coming to a close, Sher Mohammad Khan was confident of a decisive victory on the following day.[46] During the night, a fresh batch of Sikh volunteers from North East came to join them, which redoubled the courage of the Sikh forces. Guru Tegh Bahadur had spent a number of years in the North East and had a large following of disciples. It was these disciples who came as volunteers to fight for the Sikh cause. The Sikhs had spent the night in the trenches and early morning they were prepared for a hand to hand fight in which the enemy was no match to the Khalsa.[47] Khizar Khan, brother of Sher Mohammad Khan was watching the day break, when a bullet fired from the trenches struck him and he went rolling down to the ground.[48] The death of Khizar Khan created lot of confusion in the Afghan ranks and some of them started running away. Sher Mohammad Khan came out to face the Sikhs. The Sikhs rushed upon their enemy and drove away the Afghans and Ranghars before them. Nashtar Khan and Wali Mohammad Khan were both killed in the scuffle and Sher Mohammad Khan was severely wounded.[49] Sikhs were now victors of the day. The strategy adopted by the Sikhs in this battle which was not going in their favour till evening, was to spend the night lying in the trenches and be able to take a lead on them in early morning.

While the Mujhail Sikhs were fighting with the Afghans of Maler Kotla, Banda Bahadur marched upon Banur and occupied the same. The Sikhs were very jubilant and Banda Bahadur's

[46] *Ibid.*, p. 42.
[47] *Ibid.*, p. 42.
[48] *Ibid.*, p. 42, Ganda Singh, *op. cit.*, p. 53.
[49] *Ibid.*, p. 42, Ganda Singh, *op. cit.*, p. 53.

army marched few miles to receive the Sikh forces coming from Ropar side. The memorable convergence of the two Sikh forces took place between Kharar and Banur on the Ambala Ropar road.[50]

BATTLE OF CHAPARH JHIRI (SIRHIND)

The historians have all along been wrongly writing Chappar Chiri whereas the land in the area was then and still is full of ponds (chaparhs), small and big, and mangroves that had grown up on the banks of the ponds, which are called 'Jhiri' in the local dialect and the correct name for the place is 'Chaparh Jhiri'.

Banda Bahadur seems to have made some sort of a plan in his mind to consolidate his hold on nearby Muslim towns and large villages around Sirhind especially those where some executioners etc of the Gurus and their children were located. (See map attached). Banda Bahadur's smaller battles viz. Banghar dacoits, Sonepat, Kaithal, Samana, Ghuram, Thaska, Thanesar, Shahbad, Kapuri and Sadhura etc. helped him to plan for the bigger battles, the increase in the strength and field training of his volunteer force, collection of arms and ammunition etc. The winning of all these battles by Banda Bahadur created a state of helplessness and depression in the ruling Mughal officials who had not experienced defeat during the past few centuries of Mughal rule.

Wazir Khan had an army of about 20,000 men of all ranks cavalry, musketeers, archers, artillery and a train of elephants to give battle to the Sikhs and check their advance towards Sirhind besides the armies of local *mansabdars* and big *zamindars* and the

[50] *Ibid.*, p. 43.

large scale Ghazi volunteer force of Muslim militants.[51] The Sikh army strength has not been assessed by any contemporary historian, but it was far less than the Mughal army. It also had a large irregular force interested in booty and plunder. They stay on to loot when their side is winning and flee when the side is losing.[52]

Banda Bahadur had chosen a mound with mangroves on both sides and a pond in front with marshy land on the other end. He would generally watch the battle from the raised point and then personally enter the battle as and when it was so required. It was at Chaparh Jhiri about 10 kms outside Sirhind, the Mughal army came out to face the Sikhs on 22nd May 1710.[53] The mound and the mangroves and the Chaparh stand till today in memory of the historic fight of the Sikhs with Wazir Khan.

Wazir Khan had large number of elephants, mounted gunnery, archers, lancers and swordsmen. Banda Bahadur had no elephants, no artillery; his soldiers had long spears, arrows, swords and unbounded courage to avenge the assassination of their Guru's younger sons. Sikh volunteers from Doaba and Majha joined Sikh forces in the evening before the battle. The artillery of Wazir Khan inflicted heavy casualties amongst the Sikhs. But the Sikhs were able to snatch one of their main gun and thereafter hand to hand fight ensued.[54]

When the Sikhs were feeling the pressure of enemy attack, Banda Bahadur rushed to the forefront. In the words of Sohan

[51]Ganda Singh, *op. cit.*, pp. 59-60.
[52]*Ibid.*, pp. 61-62.
[53]*Ibid.*, p. 63.
[54]Deol G.S., *op. cit.*, p. 47.

Singh, "Banda rose like a hungry lion and sprang on the enemy like a bolt from the blue, the irresistible Banda Bahadur with a single sally changed the whole scene."[55] Khafi Khan says, "Money, horses, elephants fell in the hands of infidels, horsemen and footmen in large numbers fell under the swords of infidels, who pursued them as far as Sirhind, Wazir Khan fell from his horse and was captured alive."[56] "Coming face to face with Banda Bahadur Wazir Khan's head was struck off with one blow by Banda Bahadur," states Macauliffe.[57] The Mughal army ran away for their lives leaving behind vast quantities of arms and ammunition.

Wazir Khan indulged in a very petty war strategy by sending one mischievous Hindu leader with 1,000 paid men pretending that they have come over to him as they were fed up with the tyranny and injustice of Nawab. They were actually hired to kill Banda Bahadur for which handsome rewards were to be made. Banda Bahadur accepted them, allotted them a place amongst his troops knowing well that there was a trap for him. They were warned that if they indulge in any treacherous activity they shall be punished. Shortly after the start of the battle, these men were noticed to be shifting towards the enemy side. They were suitably punished along with the rest of the Mughal army.[58]

Banda Bahadur and his men carried out the last rites of the fallen Sikhs at the battle site before entering the city. The body of

[55]Sohan Singh, *op. cit.*, p. 59. "Banda Bahadur rose like a famished lion from his cave and sprang upon the enemy like a bold from the blue. His appearance encouraged the Khalsa by far the most while it struck terror amongst the enemy."

[56]Deol G.S., *op. cit.*, p. 47.

[57]*Ibid.*, p. 48.

[58]*Ibid.*, pp. 44-45.

Wazir Khan was hung from a nearby tree upside down and was also burnt afterwards.[59] The said tree still stands in the compound of a school built at that site.

Victorious Sikh army entered Sirhind on 24th May 1710 and large scale plundering went on for three days.[60] The plundering was stopped on the fourth day when Banda Bahadur entered Sirhind. He established his own government.[61] Baj Singh was appointed governor of Sirhind. Baba Ali Singh was appointed his Naib (Assistant), Fateh Singh confirmed in his post as Fauzdar of Samana. Binod Singh and Ram Singh were jointly appointed governors of Thanesar. Hindu officials were appointed in all other subordinate posts in the place of Muslim officials. The Khalsa flag was hoisted on the fort of Sirhind. The battle of Sirhind is considered as the first major battle fought and won by the Sikhs against Mughal forces.

It is a great irony that for Banda Bahadur, the tallest Indian warrior of his times, the Indian nation, the Panjab State and the Sikhs in particular have failed to give him his due. While monuments and memorials are raised every now and then for the big and the small, there is no memorial set up so far for this brave son of the Mother-land.

The place where the last rites of about 5,000 Sikh volunteer force were performed stands sanctified by the local population guarding the area of about 50 acres along side the Chaparh Jhiri, where no cultivation has since been done nor even cattle allowed to graze; lest the mortal remains of the Sikh martyrs be disturbed.

[59]Deol G.S., *op. cit.*, p. 49.
[60]*Ibid.*, p. 51.
[61]Ganda Singh, *op. cit.*, p. 72.

An Urdu couplet that used to be sung during independence movement reminds:

Shaheedon ki chitaon par lagen ge har bars mele,
watan par mitne walon ka yahi baaki nishan hoga.

INCURSIONS IN THE JAMUNA-GANGA DOAB

Banda Bahadur and his warriors marched on Saharanpur on their way to Jalalabad. Saharanpur was a principal stronghold of bigoted Mohammadans. Ali Hamid Khan was the faujdar. He, however, collected his family and valuables and fled away to Delhi the same night.[62] The residents put up a resistance but they were no match to Sikh warriors and were subjected to slaughter and plunder. A large booty fell into the hands of the Sikh soldiers.[63]

The Peerzadas of nearby Behat were notorious fanatics, and it was on the request of Hindu population, the Peerzadas were put to the sword.[64]

Sikhs now moved towards Jalalabad and a message was sent to Jalal Khan to release the Sikh prisoners and tender his submission. Jalal Khan insulted the Sikh messengers and turned them out of the town. Since Sikhs were to pass through Ambehta and Nanauta, they looted these villages. The Gujjar community of Nanauta became the worshippers of Guru Nanak. The Shaikhzadas of Nanauta put up resistance but they were severely crushed. According to a contemporary writer,

[62] *Ibid.*, p. 91.

[63] *Ibid.*, pp. 91-92.

[64] William G.R.C., *The Sikhs in Upper Doab*, Calcutta Review, LX, p. 23.
"These victims were solemnly executed after conviction on the capital charge of cow slaughter, an offence easily proved against them."

300 Shaikhzadas fell dead in the Shaikh Afzal's courtyard. The prosperous town of Nanauta was a mass of smouldering ruins and the same has been popularly named afterwards as '*phoota shahr*'.[65] Sikhs reached Jalalabad and besieged the fort. Since rains had set in and breach of the fort was not possible. The Sikh warriors made a tactical retreat and left Jalalabad.[66] Unfavourable weather and the shortage of resources were responsible for this retreat.

UPRISING IN MAJHA

Haidri Flag Crusade from Lahore

Sikhs on their own part, were only waiting since the battle of Chamkaur in December 1704, for an opportunity, to settle the old scores with their persecutors. There was a sudden eruption and the Sikh volcanic Lava flowed with such rapidity and force that it drove before it all who came in its way, Muslims or Hindus, officials or non-officials."[67]

Sayyed Aslam Khan, the Imperial Governor of Lahore was a very weak person. He behaved in a most cowardly manner and dared not leave the city to oppose the Sikhs in an open fight.[68] The Muslim religious leaders disappointed with the behaviour of Aslam Khan met near the Idgah Mosque proclaimed a *jehad* (crusade) against the Sikhs and their green flag was named 'The Haidri Flag'. The Hindu traders and Muslim in general contributed liberally to this *jehad*. Governor Aslam Khan also

[65] Ganda Singh, *op. cit.*, p. 95.
[66] *Ibid.*, p. 98.
[67] *Ibid.*, p. 101.
[68] *Ibid.*, p. 102.

deputed Mir Ataullah with a contingent of five hundred horse and one thousand foot.[69] Sikhs turned their attention at first to Batala and Kalanaur. They turned out Muslim Government officials and established their own thanas. These were rich areas and conquest thereof added much to the resources of the Sikhs. Some Sikhs went towards Lahore and ravaged the country upto Shalimar gardens.[70] Others moved towards Pathankot, occupied the city and the surrounding areas.

The crusaders took the lead under Haidri Flag and proclaimed a jehad against the Sikhs. The Sikhs had occupied the small fort named qila Bhagwant Rai. In a week's time very large number of crusaders came and besieged the fort. There was great bloodshed on both sides. As a tactical measure Sikhs moved out of the fort on a particular night cutting through the lines of crusaders and went out of their reach.[71] The jehadis were greatly disappointed and went back to Lahore.

Sikhs once again collected together at fort Kotla Begam, a few miles from Lahore and began their old customary ravages. The crusaders in order to cover up their shame at qila Bhagwant Rai once again marched against fort Kotla Begam ravaging poor villagers all along the way. They came face to face with the Sikhs at the foot of fort Kotla Begam.[72]

Sikhs came out of the enclosure and a desperate battle ensued. Sikhs had an upper hand. Panic and confusion gripped the crusaders and everybody was running away and by evening the Mohammadan force melted away into nothingness.[73] On

[69] *Ibid.*, p. 103.
[70] *Ibid.*, p. 102.
[71] *Ibid.*, p. 105.
[72] *Ibid.*, p. 107.
[73] *Ibid.*, p. 109.

way back, the crusaders stopped at fort Bilowal for night rest. The regular troops were lodged in the fort and the jehadis in the open all around the fort. Sikhs were watching their movement and were following them. During night they hid themselves in some bushes and trees. Early next morning, the Sikhs came out of their hiding places and attacked the crusaders who could not stand up to this unexpected attack and lost heavily in men and horses.[74] Sikhs were now in possession of whole of Majha and Rearki except the Lahore city.[75]

BATTLE OF RAHON

The Doaba of Bist Jullundur comprising the present districts of Jullundur and Hoshiarpur, being on the border of the province of Sirhind, which had been conquered and occupied by Banda Bahadur, was the first to be electrified with the spirit of rising and independence. In a few weeks many of the petty officials in the districts of the Jullundur Doab were turned out and Sikh Tehsildars and Thanedars were appointed in their places.[76] Shamas Khan was the faujdar of Doaba Bist Jullundur with his capital at Sultanpur. In accordance with the normal practice, Sikhs addressed a letter to Shamas Khan in the form of a *parvana* calling upon him to submit, to carry out certain reforms, and come out to receive them bringing with him all the amount held in the treasury. Shamas Khan gave an evasive reply to the messenger that he would soon come to meet the Sikhs. Shamas Khan was a clever officer and he proclaimed by beat of drum a *jehad* against the Sikhs. Khafi Khan says that more than hundred

[74] *Ibid.*, p. 110.
[75] *Ibid.*, p. 110.
[76] *Ibid.*, p. 112.

thousand men were collected and they marched out from Sultanpur with great display. (This number in a fairly small place appears to be exaggerated). Shamas Khan proceeded against the Sikhs at the head of four to five thousand horses and about thirty thousand infantry armed with match-locks and other weapons.[77] On hearing of these proceedings and the advance of Shamas Khan with such a large army and equipments of war, the Sikhs moved with all their force numbering forty to fifty thousand horse and foot.[78] As they came to the town of Rahon, about seven kos from Sultanpur, they occupied the mounds of some old brick-kilns lying to the north-west. From here Sikhs sent out patrols in all directions and issued threatening orders to the Chaudharies, revenue officials and Qanungos, calling upon them to submit.

When Shamas Khan and the crusaders came close to the Sikhs, about ten to twelve thousand balls and stones from slings came all at once rattling like hail upon the forces of Islam. The crusaders were swarming like locusts from all sides and rushing in with the cries of *Allah-u-Akbar*. Shamas Khan warned them against haste and ordered them a steady advance. After two volleys from the Sikhs, the Muslim regulars supported by forty to fifty thousand crusaders charged them. The Sikhs were heavily outnumbered therefore they thought it best to retire upon the fort of Rahon, which they had previously occupied.[79]

The fort of Rahon was invested for several days. The Sikhs rushed out of it in small parties at night and attacked the

[77] *Ibid.*, p. 115.
[78] *Ibid.*, p. 116.
[79] *Ibid.*, p. 117.

besieging forces, inflicting heavy losses upon them in men and horses. But their number was too large to be thinned or affected by these sorties. The Sikhs, therefore, thought of tricking the enemy with tactics peculiar to themselves and, in the darkness of a night, they slipped away from their entrenchments. Shamas Khan did not risk a pursuit of them beyond a few miles and was quite content with a gun and some loaded camels and oxen that fell into his hands. Apparently he felt tired and was looking for an opportunity to leave the Sikhs alone, especially since he thought of their being reinforced by the terrible Banda Bahadur, the conqueror of Sadhura, Sirhind and Saharanpur. He, therefore, ordered the breaking up of the camp and marched away from Rahon before day break and returned in triumph to Sultanpur. The crusaders were demobilized and despatched to their homes.[80]

But the Sikhs had not quitted the neighbourhood of Rahon. They were only lurking in the neighbouring bushes. In the morning, only a few hours after the evacuation, a thousand of them rushed upon Rahon and attacked the garrison, placed by Shamas Khan in the thana (fort) of Rahon, drove them out, occupied the fort and established themselves therein.[81]

This tactic of war, which is peculiarly a Sikh tactic and has so often been used by them in their wars with the Mughals, and later on with Durranis and the local officials, has generally been misunderstood and misinterpreted into a defeat. Their trick-flights were many a time mistaken for their actual flights and under this impression the enemy followed them up, but they

[80] *Ibid.*, p. 118.
[81] *Ibid.*, pp. 118-119.

were soon disillusioned on finding the Sikhs turning upon their heels, pouncing upon their pursuers and cutting them down to the last man. It was after such a practical experience that Qazi Nur Mohammad Gunjabavi, the author of the *Jangnamah* warns his co-religionists against this tactic of the Sikhs, and says:

"If defeat befalls their armies,
take it not as a defeat, oh youth.
Because it is a war-tactic of theirs.
Beware beware, of it!
Their tactic is such that in wreaking vengeance,
their defeat is changed into victory.
The army that pursues them is cut off from reinforcement.
Then they (the Sikhs) turn upon their heels, and,
even if their pursuers be 'water', they set fire to it."[82]

Qazi Noor Mohammad who has addressed Sikhs as 'dogs', 'infidels', and even worse, yet his above exposition is an exemplary understanding of the often used battle tactics of the Sikhs.

The battle of Rahon was fought on 11th October 1710 and the news reached emperor Bahadur Shah on 25th October, 1710 while he was encamped near Sonepat. In a period of a little over one year, after the arrival of Banda Bahadur in Panjab as the commander of the Sikh forces, the situation had turned into a general Sikh rising throughout eastern and south-eastern Punjab except the capital city of Lahore. After the occupation of Rahon, the Sikhs moved on to Jullundur. The pathans of this place were so terrified that they found safety in running away from it and unwittingly fell into the hands of the Sikhs without any

[82] *Ibid.*, pp. 119-120.

resistance at all from the officials and residents. Hoshiarpur followed suit and like all other of the neighbourhood, its rulers acknowledged the authority of the conquerors. Thus, before long, practically whole of the Bist Jullundur Doab came under the sway of the Sikhs.

To summarize the whole situation at this stage, it stood thus: there was general Sikh rising throughout the eastern and south-eastern Panjab, except the city of Lahore which was held by the Imperial Governor. The whole of Majha, the Rearki and Kandi as far as Pathankot lay prostrate at the feet of Sikhs. Jamuna-Ganga plains had been overrun and to the south of Sutlej Sikhs had complete mastery over the territory of Sirhind, from Machhiwara to Karnal. They penetrated into the province of Delhi proper and according to Iradat Khan there was no noble man daring enough to march from Delhi against them.

EMPEROR BAHADUR SHAH MARCHES AGAINST SIKHS

"If Bahadur Shah had not quitted the Deccan, which he did in AD 1710 and marched towards the Panjab with all his Imperial forces, there is every reason to think that the whole of Hindustan would have been subdued by these invaders (Sikhs)", said Malcolm in the *Sketch of Sikhs*.[83]

The news of Sikh outbreak under Banda Singh Bahadur was received by emperor Bahadur Shah on 30th May, 1710 while at Ajmer. He had come to Rajputana to reduce the refractory chiefs Raja Jai Singh Kachhwahya and Raja Ajit Singh Rathore. The alarming news from Panjab changed the situation. Various

[83]Malcolm, *Sketch of Sikhs*, London, 1812, p. 79.

reports of the newswriters and loud cries of muslims of Sirhind, Peerzadas of Sumana and Sadhura who had waited on him at Ajmer on 22nd June, 1710.[84]

The popular rising of the Sikhs, very near to the capital was considered more serious and of far-reaching consequences that the pending quarrel with the Rajputs, who even if left in quiet possession of their hereditary country were not likely to be encouraged to further aggression.

On receipt of the news of Mughal emperor advancing to Panjab with large armies to crush the Sikh movement, Banda Bahadur being aware of the situation that with his meagre resources of men and materials could not stand against the Mughal imperial armies led by their emperor. He, therefore, sought help from Rajputs, who were closer to Panjab and with whom he had some contacts. It is understood that he contacted Raja Jai Singh of Amber and Raja Ajit Singh of Jodhpur and ruler of Jawalapur seeking their help in the hour of his need. But unfortunately none of the Rajputs, who have had their grouse against the Mughals still were not prepared to come to Banda Bahadur's help.[85]

Bahadur Shah ordered Asad Khan governor of Delhi to mobilize an army for immediate advance against the Sikhs. He ordered Khan Dauran of Oudh, Amin Khan faujdar of Moradabad, Khan Jehan Nazim of Allahabad and Abdullah Khan of Barha to join him in the projected expedition. Emperor also left Ajmer and moved towards Panjab. The imperial army that arrived on 7th August was dispatched against the Sikhs under command of Feroz Khan Mewati.[86]

[84]Ganda Singh, *op. cit.*, p. 125.
[85]Sagoo H.K., *Banda Bahadur,* p. 83.
[86]Ganda Singh, *op. cit.*, p. 127.

Such was the scare that no one in the imperial army was allowed to halt in Delhi, nor any relation allowed to come to the camp. Further to eliminate any disguised Sikhs amongst the bearded Hindus in the royal camp, an order was issued on 8th September 1710, that all Hindus employed in the imperial offices were to shave off their beards. Hindu officials immediately obeyed the royal orders.[87] Emperor also ordered that an imperial army of 60,000 horsemen be kept ready for action against Sikhs.

The Sikh forces at this time were distributed all over the country in garrisons and detachments for duties at Sirhind, Suman, Thanesar, Sadhura etc. Many were busy in their own areas in Majha, Rearki and Jullundur Doab. Banda Bahadur and his leading officers had moved only a few days earlier against Shamas Khan of Sultanpur. Thus Binod Singh and Ram Singh were to bear the brunt of the battle with imperial forces.[88]

In the neighbourhood of chhichhra Sikh army was able to drive back the Mughal army under Mahabat Khan. The Sikh forces were greatly outnumbered by the imperial forces commanded by Feroz Khan Mewati and were defeated. The dead and dying Sikhs were treated with every indignity. Carts loaded with three hundred heads of Sikhs were sent to the emperor.[89] The Sikhs retired from Thanesar and retreated towards Sadhura to fall back on Lohgarh if necessary.

Bayzid Khan with Shamas Khan and Umar Khan marched against the Sikhs in Sirhind. Sikhs being greatly outnumbered retired to the fort of Sirhind. Emperor ordered the siege of the

[87] *Ibid.*, p. 128.
[88] *Ibid.*, p. 131.
[89] *Ibid.*, p. 132.

fort and for which a force was dispatched. The fort had fallen into the hands of Shamas Khan and he had dispatched the heads of 300 Sikhs killed in the battle to the emperor, which were received at Sadhura.[90]

THE BATTLES OF SADHURA AND LOHGARH JUNE 1710 TO DECEMBER 1711

Historians and newswriters have been calling Banda Bahadur a great magician. This had a very depressing effect on the Emperor and his commanders.

On 4th December, 1710 Rustam Dil Khan and other commanders moved towards Sadhura fort to face the Sikhs. They were faced with great shower of arrows, rockets and musket balls. Khafi Khan says that, "The Sikhs in their faqir dress struck terror in the royal troops. The number of dead and dying of imperial troops was so large that for a time it seemed that they were losing ground. Nephew of Feroze Khan Mewati was killed and his son wounded. Most of the Rustam Dil Khan's followers could not stand the on-rush and were scattered.[91] But soon after rest of the imperial troops arrived and outnumbered the Sikhs. Kamwar Khan, the author of Tazkirat-i-Salatin-i-Chughtaiya was then present with the troops and saw that everyone of the cursed Sikhs came out of the entrenchment, challenged the imperial troops and after great struggle and trial fell under the swords of the Ghazis. With the sunset, the Sikhs retreated towards the eastern mountains and fell back upon the fort of Lohgarh on 5th December 1710.[92]

[90] *Ibid.*, p. 134.
[91] *Ibid.*, p. 136.
[92] *Ibid.*, p. 137.

The strength of the Mughal armies, both the Mughal Imperial Army and the armies of the various other governors and generals taken together were approximately 2 lakhs combatants, horsemen and lakh or so non-combatant camp followers etc. As against this strength the fighting force of the Sikhs which could be collected at this short notice was less than 15,000 horsemen and those on foot.

Mughal armies now moved on to the other bank of Som *nadi* (rainy season water stream) facing Lohgarh. The rivulet was running very low on water due to winter season. The Emperor also arrived at site on 9th December, 1710, within sight of Lohgarh which lay on a high summit.[93] The fort was very closely infested with over 60,000 imperial troops, horse and foot, reinforced by large number of plunderers and others. Lohgarh was considered so strong and inaccessible by the Mughals that Bahadur Shah did not attack the Sikhs in their fortress and resolved to seem inactive for sometime to tempt them to an engagement. When Munim Khan arrived within a shot of their entrenchments the Sikhs began a cannonade from their works while bodies of their infantries on the heights rained with rockets, musketry, and arrows. The Wazir more out of jealousy of his military fame than fear of the Emperor's displeasure ventured for once to disobey the imperial orders and ordered an attack. When some of the Mughal officials went close to the mud-fort, a canon ball from a tamarind tree on the top of a hillock threw the group in disorder.[94]

At the time of evening prayer, Munim Khan sure of having the Sikh chief in his power, ordered his troops to cease the attack

[93] *Ibid.*, p. 138.
[94] *Ibid.*, p. 140.

and to lie upon their arms in their present position till morning should enable them to finish it with success. He left Rustam Dil Khan and his troops to surround the hill and the fort of Lohgarh and returned to the Royal Camp to report the emperor the course of events. The besieged Sikhs had no stores of foods and fodder in the fort of Lohgarh and they feared to be reduced to great extremities in no time. From the top of their fort they bargained with signs of their hands and eyes with the grain dealers of the royal armies and bought what they could from them at 2-3 rupees a seer of grain. They threw their sheets from above and pulled them up with ropes.[95]

Banda Bahadur decided to move out of the Lohgarh fort on the night of 11th December. An explosion of a cannon made out of a tamarind tree which was filled with powder was blown to pieces as they were just about to retreat. The Mughal soldiers lying low for the morning to rise did not obstruct the marching out of the Lohgarh Fort by Banda Bahadur and his troops in the middle of night and escape towards the mountains of the Barfi Raja of Nahan.[96]

In the morning when the Mughal commanders with their soldiers arrived at the fort, and to their utter dismay, they found total silence and inside the fort were about a dozen injured persons and the alleged Gulab Singh besides some five elephants, three pieces of cannons and some silver poles etc. The five elephants mentioned above also seem to be a fictional concoction as the Sikh armies in the period of Banda Bahadur had no elephant at all with them.

[95] *Ibid.*, pp. 143-144.
[96] *Ibid.*, pp. 144-145.

The foundations and area was extensively dug up to find out some hidden treasure and about 8 lakhs rupees are alleged to have been recovered. This assessment has been an exaggerated amount as the amount realized at the time of each and every battle was distributed among the soldiers and only a very small amount was kept for contingencies. When this news was conveyed to the Emperor, he was totally displeased and disappointed with some of his commanders. He is said to have addressed his commanders that: "a pack of wild hounds could not catch a jackal". Emperor broke his camp and moved towards Lahore via Ropar, Hoshiarpur etc.[97]

Note: The story of the fall of Sadhura and Lohgarh as narrated above taken primarily from Mughal news reports of Khafi Khan and Kamwar Khan said to be present with the troops suffers from various inaccuracies and distortions. The Sadhura and Lohgarh have been examined number of times during the last five years as a committee formed by Shiromani Gurudwara Parbandhak Committee, Amritsar for the establishment of a memorial of Banda Bahadur at these places. I was appointed Convenor of that Committee and hence had to examine these two places from various aspects and the recorded historical accounts of the battles. The various inaccuracies and distortions are as under:

1. Macauliffe has stated that Banda Bahadur's forces fought with great bravery and captured the fort at Sadhura and levelled it to the ground. Couple of historians have mentioned this point but no body has shared the views of Macauliffe. If any fort existed it would have been put to use by the Sikh forces and the question of destroying it was meaningless.

[97] *Ibid.*, pp. 145-146.

2. When Banda Bahadur occupied Sadhura, there was no fort as such with the Mughal authorities at Sadhura. It could be that there was a wall around the city, but no signs of it in the form of parts of the wall or the foundations etc. are available. There are ruins of an old abandoned fort slightly away from the town which obviously belongs to the early centuries of Hindu period. It is likely that Sikh forces had dug some trenches as it is recorded that they would come out of the entrenchments and fight bravely with the Mughals.

3. The statement that emperor's camp had within its sight the Lohgarh fort on a high summit, is incorrect. Even today by standing on the partly standing walls of the fort, the Som *nadi* and its opposite bank are not visible. The situation being talked of is 300 years old when the forests were very dense as compared to today when large scale deforestation has taken place.

4. The Lohgarh fort being called mud-fort by the newswriters is incorrect as all the walls of this fort have been built with one side chiseled stone and the chiseled side being kept towards the outer side. There are no signs of any white building or ruins of a building that could be observed from the royal camp. In fact, even at present and in broad daylight the remains of the fort are not visible from the bank of Som *nadi*.

5. There is no fort at Sitaragarh as there are remains only of a thatched hut from where Banda Bahadur used to survey the entire area and the position of Mughal troops. The top of the Sitaragarh is a kilometer away from the Lohgarh fort as crow flies, but to this date spoken words from Sitaragarh are heard at Lohgarh and likewise from Lohgarh to Sitaragarh due to some acoustic phenomenon.

6. The Mughal forces moved from Sadhura to Lohgarh area from 7th to 9th with the emperor reaching bank of Som *nadi* near Lohgarh on 9th December, 1710. There was no difficulty in the way of Sikh forces to collect rations etc. upto 6th December. The Sikhs left Lohgarh on the night of 10th December, 1710. The stay of the main body of Sikh troops from Sadhura was only for three days at Lohgarh. The statement that the besieged Sikhs had no stores of foods and fodder in the fort of Lohgarh and they feared to be reduced to great extremities in no time is an incorrect and frivolous statement. There was no pressure on Sikh troops at Lohgarh and the lines of communication had remained open till 6th of December, 1710. Moreover, the Sikh troops always kept emergency ration of roasted grams for a few days for themselves and for their horses. The story that they bargained with signs with the grain dealers of royal army and bought what they could from them for 2 to 3 rupees a seer of grain, is a fictional fable in view of the existing situation.

7. The story of Gulab Singh, a trader, who volunteered to wear the clothes of Banda Bahadur and move on the ramparts so that Banda Bahadur and his troops could walk out of the fort in incognito is incorrect. In the month of December in a jungle the sunlight becomes almost extinct by 5 p.m., hence Gulab Singh moving on the ramparts could not be visible to the Mughal emperor and his commanders. The story is a pure and simple fictional concoction.

8. Sikh armies during Banda Bahadur's time had kept only horses, may be some camels, but there is no reference any where of elephants having been kept. As such finding five elephants in Lohgarh is a fanciful reconstruction.

On the morning of 11th December, 1710, the Mughal commanders went to the fort to arrest Banda Bahadur and his force, but found to their dismay, Banda Bahadur and his soldiers had already left Lohgarh fort on the previous night and only a few wounded and dying Sikhs and some families of a nearby village who had taken shelter were there. Taking the wounded Sikhs as prisoners, the Mughal commanders and nobles with their heads hanging came down to the emperor.[98] Orders were issued on the same day to the Rajas (zamindars of Srinagar and Nahan) calling upon them to seize the Sikh leader and dispatch him to the royal presence.[99] Emperor by slow marches, his movement hampered by rains, reached Ropar on 30th April and Lahore on 11th August, 1711.[100]

Banda Bahadur conquered and set up the Sikh state over a vast area in over a year's time. The same was, however, taken back by the Mughals in three months' time.

SUBMISSION OF HILL CHIEFS TO BANDA BAHADUR

Battles of Bahrampur, Batala etc.

The escape of Banda Bahadur and Sikhs and the evacuation of the fort of Lohgarh cannot be considered a defeat for the Sikhs. It was rather a defeat for the emperor and his marauding forces, whose every effort to capture or kill the Sikh leader had hopelessly failed. He escaped, sword in hand, cutting through the lines of over 60,000 horse and foot.[101] He had, of course,

[98] *Ibid.*, pp. 145-146.
[99] *Ibid.*, p. 147.
[100] *Ibid.*, p. 150.
[101] *Ibid.*, p. 151.

conquered six districts of Punjab from Panipat to Lahore, but it was purely a military occupation and it was not an indisputable complete mastery over that area. Banda Bahadur was not dejected by the loss of his stronghold and treasure. These, he knew, were not the main sources of his strength.[102] His strength lay mainly in the indomitable spirit of the Khalsa, on whom, he knew, he could safely depend.[103] Within a fortnight of the departure from Lohgarh, he had issued circular letters *hukamnamas* to the Khalsa throughout the country calling them to join him at once.[104] Immediately on receipt of Banda Bahadur's letters Sikhs from all parts of Panjab assembled at Kiratpur.

Raja Bhim Chand of Kahlur had been a source of great annoyance to Guru Gobind Singh. A *parvana* as usual was sent to him to submit to the Khalsa.[105] Bhim Chand started securing help from neighbouring leading zamindars and other hill rajas and strengthened the fortress of Bilaspur. His main force was thirteen hundred *Mians*. In the Sikh attack, most of the *Mians* were killed.[106] They were buried in thirteen ditches. The town yielded immense booty to the Sikhs. The defeat of Bhim Chand unnerved most of the Rajput chieftains of Shivalik hills and they readily came to the Sikhs, offered their allegiance and paid *nazrana* and tribute in the Sikh treasury.[107] Next to fall in line was Raja Sidh Sain of Mandi. Here Guru Gobind Singh had

[102] *Ibid.*, p. 151.
[103] *Ibid.*, p. 151.
[104] *Ibid.*, p. 152.
[105] *Ibid.*, p. 154.
[106] *Ibid.*, p. 155.
[107] *Ibid.*, p. 155.

stayed for some time and a large Gurudwara is built on the river bank and some relics of the Guru ji are preserved therein.

Raja Bhup Parkash was arrested by the Mughals and brought to the Royal camp on 22nd December, 1710. Khafi Khan says that Bhup Parkash (Barfi Raja) was sent to Delhi in an iron cage for his not being able to catch Banda Bahadur. Mughal sappers dug out at various places in the Lohgarh fort for his hidden treasure. It is alleged that they were able to locate 8 lakhs of rupees and gold mohars. This seems to be a morale boosting exaggeration as most of the booty collected by Sikh forces was distributed amongst the Khalsa immediately on its receipt. Emperor Bahadur Shah reached Ropar on 17th March, 1711 and reached Lahore on 11th August, 1711.

From Mandi Banda Bahadur proceeded towards Kullu and the story goes that he fell in the hands of Raja Man Singh of Kullu. The Raja imprisoned him in a cage, probably with a view to hand him over to Mughal emperor Bahadur Shah. Banda Bahadur in the meantime managed to escape from his confinement and made his way to Mandi.[108] This story does not seem to be true as Banda Bahadur had his forces with him and when he went to Chamba from Mandi via Kullu, he had a sizeable number of Sikh force with him which was left at the Kotla fort when Banda Bahadur went to Chamba with a few of his confidantes. During a visit to the Kotla fort on top of a hill near Nurpur this was a common story that Banda's army stayed here for some months in Kotla fort. So story of his having been arrested by the Raja of Kullu seems to be a fabrication. In Chamba Banda Bahadur married a Chamba girl, and he had a

[108] *Ibid.*, p. 159.

son named Ajit Singh born towards the end of year 1711. In the beginning of February/March 1711 that is within three months of the fall of Lohgarh, Banda Bahadur came to Raipur and Bahrampur and began to extend his influence in the direction of Gurdaspur.[109] Bayzid Khan, faujdar of Jammu was near Raipur. His nephew Shamas Khan had also come there to him. On the news of appearance of the Sikhs in the area, one thousand five hundred horses were gathered with all haste for the protection of Raipur. Bayzid Khan and Shamas Khan moved out at the head of nine hundred horse, and having gone half-way they started indulging in hunting etc rather than preparing to fight with the Sikhs.[110]

Shamas Khan went out to meet the Sikhs, but was easily tricked by Sikhs by their old Rahon tactics. It seems that they pretended to fly at the sight of Shamas Khan, who, inspite of the warning of his uncle Bayzid Khan hastened to pursue them at close quarters. They had not gone very far when the Sikhs, all of a sudden, sharply turned upon their heels and pounced upon their pursuers.

In an instant the battle ensued with all its fury and the Mohammadans were driven back line by line, leaving heaps of them dead and wounded. When Bayzid Khan and Shamas Khan saw that scales were turning against them they rushed to oppose the advancing Sikhs like Baj Singh and others. Baj Singh and Fateh Singh came out to meet them. Shamas Khan was wounded and he rushed on Baj Singh with naked sword. Baj Singh received the sword upon his shield and gave him so

[109] *Ibid.*, p. 160.
[110] *Ibid.*, p. 161.

heavy a blow that Shamas Khan's sword fell down from his hands. Pahar Singh fell upon Shamas Khan before he could attack Baj Singh a second time, and so strongly hit him that his head rolled on the ground. Bayzid Khan was also mortally wounded and died a few days later.[111]

With the fall of their leaders, confusion spread in the Muslim ranks and they took to their heels. With great difficulty they were able to get the dead bodies of Shamas Khan and Bayzid Khan. The whole of the camp equipage of faujdar of Jammu and Shamas Khan fell in the hands of Sikhs who overran the town of Raipur and Bahrampur and advanced on the parganas of Kalanaur and Batala.[112]

Banda Bahadur arrived at the Tank of Achal, two kos to the east of Batala, and on the following day turned his attention to the city. The inhabitants shut the gates and prepared themselves for its defence. Shaikh-ul-Hind with his followers went out of Hathi Gate to meet Banda Bahadur. He put up a bold stand, but he was overpowered and slain. The Sikh forces broke open the gates and entered the city. Part of the city including many palatial buildings got perished in the fire.[113]

Banda Bahadur desired to advance on Lahore, but having come to know that he was being followed by Mughal army, he sacked Aurangabad and Pasrur.

Mohd. Amin Khan and Rustam Dil Khan combined their forces and encircled Banda Bahadur on three sides. Banda Bahadur, by his fertile mind in expedients, extricated himself without any loss. He kept moving on their outskirts and

[111] *Ibid.*, p. 163.
[112] *Ibid.*, p. 164.
[113] *Ibid.*, p. 165.

avoided direct confrontation. When he had given them a slip, he suddenly sailed forth from the opposite side near Parol and Kathua, and fell upon the troops of Rustam Dil Khan. All efforts of Rustam Dil Khan failed to stem the tide of advancing Sikhs. They would cut through Mughal lines and escape unhurt massacring imperial troops and destroying everything that came their way.[114]

Rustam Dil Khan could not take the defeat in a sporting manner, he perpetuated extreme excesses against the civil population of Parol and Kathua giving them to his soldiers in lieu of pay, who would, in turn, sell them as wretches in the horse market of Lahore.[115]

An imperial order was issued for wholesale massacre of Sikhs wherever found. This gave the mad fanatics an official encouragement for their excesses which had no bounds. The oppression was carried out most indiscriminately and many people were murdered and persecuted on charge of being Sikhs or their supporters and sympathizers, as has been reported in *Tarikh-i-Muhammad Shahi*. The emperor re-published the royal *farman* calling upon all the Hindus in the royal camp to shave off their beards. The hair and the beard were considered to be the only visible distinction between the Sikhs and Hindus. Sikhs would under no circumstances, even under pain of death, cut or shave their beards.[116]

Bahadur Shah reached Lahore on 23 June, 1711. He did not reside in the fort, but set up his camp at Anwala near the bank of river Ravi.[117] He had developed some mental ailment and his

[114] *Ibid.*, p. 167.
[115] *Ibid.*, p. 168.
[116] *Ibid.*, p. 169.
[117] *Ibid.*, p. 174.

health started failing and his decisions becoming more and more erratic. He expired on 28th February 1712.[118] Death of Bahadur Shah was followed by usual struggle amongst his sons for the throne during 14th to 17th March, 1712. The elephant of Azim-us-Shan being wounded by a cannon ball that it threw itself down into the Ravi where prince and the animal were swallowed by quick sand. Ultimately, Jahandar Shah having surprised and slain his remaining brothers, Jahan Shah and Rafi-us-Shan in a battle fought on the 27th-28th March, 1712 ascended the Mughal throne on 29th March, 1712.[119]

The period of struggle for the imperial throne and the disturbed state of affairs at Lahore and Delhi from February 1712 to summer of 1713 when Abdul Samad Khan laid siege of Sadhura was very favourable for the reestablishment of the power of the Khalsa.[120] Banda Bahadur had reappeared in the neighbourhood of Bahrampur, killed Shamas Khan and mortally wounded his uncle Bayzid Khan, the faujdar of Jammur. The Khalsa army overran the parganas of Kalanaur and Batala.[121]

On the death of Bahadur Shah, Mohd. Amin Khan returned to Lahore to take part in the struggle for succession. Banda Bahadur availed himself of the opportunity and occupied Sadhura without any loss of time. After capturing Sadhura, fort of Lohgarh was repaired and made usable.[122] The agility with which he moved in the craggy mountains appears to have been remarkable.

[118] *Ibid.*, p. 179.
[119] *Ibid.*, p. 180.
[120] *Ibid.*, p. 180.
[121] *Ibid.*, p. 180.
[122] *Ibid.*, p. 181.

SIEGE OF SADHURA AND LOHGARH

After Jahandar Shah taking over as the Mughal emperor, Amin Khan and Zain-ud-din Khan, faujdar of Sirhind, were sent back to continue campaign against the Sikhs. Besides the imperial army, whatever troops that could be spared from nearby area were also sent. For several months, these two commanders maintained a close siege of Sadhura and Lohgarh fort, but they failed to make any effect on the besieged Sikh troops and the half-hearted repeated attacks were repulsed by the Sikh forces. In December 1712, Jahandar Shah moved towards Agra to oppose advance of Farrukh Siyar. Amin Khan and his troops were withdrawn and the expedition against the Sikhs remained virtually suspended.[123] Jahandar Shah was defeated in January 1712 and murdered in February 1713.[124]

The reign of Farrukh Siyar which began with a series of murders and famine in north India has been notorious period for the most cruel policies adopted against the Sikhs.[125]

Banda Bahadur availed of the lull in fighting and raised a fort of sufficiently large size close to the town of Sadhura. Besides maintaining his position against opposing Faujdar of Sirhind, he had got a deep trench dug around the fort and a 10 feet high mud-wall raised from the dug-out earth and water filled in the trench from a nearby canal. He had also raised four 35 feet high towers at four corners to watch the movements of Mughal forces. In the battle of Sadhura in July 1713, three watch towers were demolished, but the fourth escaped

[123] *Ibid.*, p. 183.
[124] *Ibid.*, p. 183.
[125] Miss Corner, *History of India and China*, p. 296.

demolition and stands intact to this day, in the midst of houses built all around.[126]

The fighting spirit of the Sikh garrison in the fort Sadhura was remarkable. They would continue their fire upon the enemy even while they were cooking and eating unmindful of the inclemency of the weather. Zain-ud-din brought a heavy gun in position and opened incessant fire on the Sikhs. The Sikh garrison, out of mere bravado, resolved to remove this gun so as no one should hear its sound or learn where it had gone. They dug out a subterranean passage exactly opposite the position where the gun stood. On a dark rainy night, where nothing could be seen, the Sikhs found their opportunity to drag the gun away. At mid night they pierced through the remaining wall before the earlier passage. Some Sikh soldiers swam across the moth, and reached the gun. They tied rope firmly to the gun carriage and came back to their own positions. The cannon was getting pulled towards their side when unfortunately the ropes broke off and the gun carriage fell apart causing a large noise. Besiegers were really surprised as to where the gun had gone. After much search, the gun was located lying in the ditch. Zain-ud-din collected couple of hundred followers who were given Rs. 50/- each to pull back the gun to a place of safety.[127] This example shows the spirit with which the Khalsa volunteer force was fighting against the Mughal empire.

After securing himself on the throne of Delhi, Farrukh Siyar directed his attention to the affairs of Panjab. He appointed

[126](i) Ganda Singh, *op. cit.*, p. 183.
(ii) *Akhabarat-i-Darbar-i-Mualla*, Nov. 25 1710, *Panjab Past and Present,* 1707-18, vol. xviii-II, October 1984, p. 44.

[127]*Ibid.*, p. 184.

Samad Khan as governor of Panjab on 22nd February 1713 and his son Zakariya Khan as Faujdar of Jammu. The directions from the emperor to Samad Khan were "to expel Banda from Sadhura, or if possible, to destroy him altogether."[128]

When Samad Khan arrived at Sadhura the siege laid by Zain-ud-Din Khan had not made any progress. Banda himself was at Lohgarh and his main force at Sadhura. The combined forces of Samad Khan and other Mughal commanders surrounded the fort of Sadhura from all sides.[129]

To give support to the troops at Sadhura, Banda Bahadur sent out three or four sections every other day or even on successive days. When the besieged Sikh army saw the arrival of Sikh troops from Lohgarh, they would rush out on all four sides and boldly strike the Mughal armies and cut down many a Mughal soldiers. But these attacks were not making any major effect on the Mughal armies. The stores of ammunition and food stocks were getting depleted. Banda Bahadur, once again decided to withdraw his forces to Lohgarh. In the first week of October 1713, the Sikh forces, in the middle of a dark night, rushed and made a determined sally upon the Zimindari militia. The hired levies could not stand against the death defying Sikh warriors. The desperate Khalsa cut through their lines and escaped with very little loss.[130]

During the long siege, when Banda Bahadur sent Sikh forces to relieve those at Sadhura, a division of the imperial troops was sent to oppose them. The fight cost the life of imperial commander Baqa Beg Khan and large number of his troops.[131]

[128] *Ibid.*, p. 186.
[129] *Ibid.*, p. 187.
[130] *Ibid.*, p. 188-89.
[131] *Ibid.*, p. 189.

Abd-us-Samad Khan and Zain-ud-din Khan followed the Sikhs to Lohgarh and were surprised to see the elaborate preparations for resistance.

Sikhs had made fifty two defensive entrenchments all around the Lohgarh fort. These entrenchments with small supporting walls were made in a manner that each supported the other. The forces moving up the hillock to the fort were to receive deadly fire throughout his advance, from every entrenchment. The fear of Sikhs might turn back from the fort was keeping the Mughal commanders and their forces ill at ease. After a few days Sikh forces moved away in the Haripur reserve forests. The fall of Sadhura and escape of Banda Bahadur was reported to the emperor on 9th October, 1713.[132]

KIRI PATHAN, ROPAR AND BATALA

The decline of Sikh power and the official persecution of Sikhs gave an impetus to the Mohammadans, officials and others all over the country to persecute them remorselessly. The oppression was felt most in Majha and Rearki where almost every Muslim considered it his duty to add to the miseries of the Sikhs. The parganas of Kalanaur, Batala and Kahnuwan in the present district of Gurdaspur had been the stronghold of Mohammadan power.[133] Most of the leading Muslims fanning Muslim bigotry against the Sikhs, belonged to village of Kiri Pathan.

The Sikhs of the neighbourhood, who were greatly exasperated by the tyrannical attitude of local Muslim population, collected under the leadership of Jagat Singh and

[132] *Ibid.*, p. 190.
[133] *Ibid.*, p. 192.

on 27 March, 1714 fell upon the village and entered the garhi of the Pathans. The resistance offered by the Pathans was overpowered and their leader was slain. Sufficient booty was also obtained.[134]

Banda Bahadur was awaiting his time in Jammu hills at a place now called Dera Baba Banda Singh Bahadur, waiting for a favourable opportunity to strike a blow for the independence of his people and for re-establishment of his power. No details of his activities from October 1713 to February 1715 are available except that he solemnized a second marriage with Sahib Kaur, daughter of a Khatri of Wazirabad.

The allegations raised by Giani Gian Singh that Banda proclaimed himself a Guru, that he visited Golden Temple, Amritsar and his disobedience of Mata Sundri who was prompted by Farrukh Siyar, are the allegations which lack authenticity. There is absolutely nothing in the contemporary or earliest available records, official diaries and chronologies, state and family histories, personal memoirs etc. to show that any negotiations at that time were carried out between Farrukh Siyar and Mata Sundri. Banda Bahadur introduced a new and additional form of salutation "Fateh Darshan" which is available on some of his *hukamnamas*. Some later historians uncharitable towards Banda Bahadur have called it a war cry in replacement of "Wahe Guru ji ka Khalsa Wahe Guru ji ki Fateh" which also has been a form of salutation and not a war cry. New salutation appears to have been dropped for having not been appreciated by the Khalsa.[135]

[134] *Ibid.*, p. 193.
[135] *Ibid.*, p. 195.

There are other instances where the Sikhs did not like some new thing and the same were dropped, e.g. the initial legend for the Sikh coinage was dropped and a new legend selected. Sikhs had lost their strong-holds and their stores of food and fodder in the plains, hence it became difficult for them to subsist. Therefore, Sikhs had no other course left but to retire to the hills.

Sikhs under Banda Bahadur reappeared in the plains from the direction of Jammu and marched towards Kalanaur. The faujdar Suhrab Khan of Kalanaur and others collected a large force of mercenaries, religious zealots and levies from the parganas of its neighbourhood, but with the very first blow of Sikhs they were scattered to the winds. Some fled from the field, others died in combat.[136]

Passing through Achal, Banda Singh marched towards Batala. The faujdar of Batala Shaikh Dayan, came out to encounter the Sikh force. In a six-hour battle, the locals could not stand against the Sikhs. Batala and its neighbourhood was occupied.

BATTLE OF GURDAS NANGAL

The news of Sikh advances reaching Mughal capital, created great alarm. An expedition consisting of many Muslims and even Hindu commanders was being collected at Lahore to fight under the command of Samad Khan whose arrival was awaited. Banda Bahadur was not unaware of the above preparations by the Mughal government. He, therefore, decided to set up a mud-fort at Kot Mirza Jan, a small village between Kalanaur and Batala as an escape route on the lines of Lohgarh into the forest area behind Kot Mirza Jan.[137]

[136] *Ibid.*, pp. 195-196.
[137] *Ibid.*, p. 199.

But before the fort could be raised for occupation, the combined Mughal force under the command of Abdul Samad Khan and his deputy Arif Beg suddenly fell upon the Sikhs. It appears that the Mughal forces were keeping track of Banda Bahadur's movements when he reappeared from Jammu side and marched towards Kalanaur. Ghulam Hussain, author of *Siyar-ul-Mutakhiran* states that Banda Bahadur stood his ground to the amazement of all and in the first engagement fought so heroically that he was very near giving a total defeat to the imperial army. The Mughals were pursuing Banda Bahadur and his men very vigorously. He withdrew from post to post like a savage of wilderness from thicket to thicket losing endlessly his men and occasioning losses to his pursuers. According to Khafi Khan, "The infidels fought so fiercely that the army of Islam was nearly overpowered and they over and over again showed the greatest daring but they had no place of defence and were, therefore, forced to evacuate their positions and fall back upon the village of Gurdas Nangal, now a heap of ruins, known as 'Bande Wali Theh' lying one mile to the west of the present village of Gurdas Nangal.[138]

The Sikhs took shelter in the *ihata* of Bhai Duni Chand's haveli. The enclosure had a fairly strong wall around it. Banda Bahadur made every effort to strengthen his defences and collect stores of ration and ammunition to keep the enemy at a respectable distance from his fortification. He surrounded it by a moat filled with water from the neighbouring canal. He cut the imperial canal called 'shahi nahar' and other streams and allowed the water to spread and form a quagmire around the

[138] *Ibid.*, p. 201.

place so that enemy could not easily come close to the enclosure.[139]

Emperor Farrukh Siyar on 17th April 1715 wrote to Abdul Samad Khan to follow the Sikhs to their new positions. He asked Itmad-ud-daula to write to Abdul Samad Khan to kill or imprison the Sikh chief and his followers.[140] The enclosure containing the Sikhs was immediately surrounded and blockaded. The besiegers kept so watchful a guard that not a blade of grass nor a grain of corn could find its way in.

Occasionally, Abdul Samad Khan and his son Zakariya Khan at the head of several thousand troops of their own and forces of their allies attempted to storm the Sikh positions, but their attempts were defeated by the comparatively small number of Sikhs who showed greatest tenacity in their defence.[140] Mohammad Qasim, author of *Ibratnama* who was in the service of Arif Beg Khan writes: "The brave and daring deeds of the infernal Sikhs were wonderful. Twice or thrice every day some forty or fifty of the black faced Sikhs came out of their enclosure to gather grass for their cattle and when the combined forces of imperialists went to oppose them they (Sikhs) made an end of the Mughals with arrows, muskets and small swords and disappeared. Such was the terror of the Sikhs and fear of the sorceries of the Sikh chief that the commander of the army prayed that God might so ordain things that Banda Bahadur should seek his safety in his flight from the Garhi.[141]

Abd-us Samad Khan utilized the reinforcement brought by Qamr-ud-din to further strengthen the reinforcements and to

[139] *Ibid.*, p. 202.
[140] *Ibid.*, p. 203.
[141] *Ibid.*, p. 204.

eliminate any chance of Sikhs breaking the siege. The area was divided into four sections commanded by four senior commanders Abd-us-Samad Khan, Qamr-ud-din, Zakriya Khan, and the faujdars and zamindars. United efforts being necessary, the tents were pitched close together all round the fort and rope was joined to rope. Slowly and slowly, unnoticed by the Sikhs, they closed all the openings between each shelter, and before the Sikhs were aware of it, they were surrounded as if by a wall.[142] The Sikhs on several occasions showed the greatest boldness and daring to sweep the obstacles away and carried away from the besiegers camp whatever they could lay their hands on.

So bold and indomitable were the Guru's followers that they impressed their adversaries with the greatest respect for their fighting qualities. It was feared that the garrison might, by a sortie *en masse* and by sacrificing themselves, secure the escape of their leader Banda Bahadur.[143] Thus, the siege and the struggle continued for several months. There were considerable losses on both sides.[144] The losses of the Sikhs were irreplaceable whereas the losses of the Mughals were replenished by fresh soldiers. With all these additions to the siege, Abd-us Samad Khan had lost hope of success against so determined and valiant a foe. All his efforts to approach the gate and the walls of the Sikh enclosures had failed. The only alternative left to him was to approach it by underground means. He, therefore, ordered to drive subterranean passages towards the corners of the *ihata*.[145]

[142] *Ibid.*, p. 205.
[143] *Ibid.*, p. 206.
[144] *Ibid.*, p. 206.
[145] *Ibid.*, p. 206.

This was comparatively successful. Before Abd-us-Samad Khan's approaches had reached the main gate, Qamr-ud-din Khan succeeded in capturing the ditch and a bastion, from which the musketery fire of the garrison had caused considerable damage. Zakariya Khan obtained possession of the second gate, the one chiefly used by the garrison. The Sikhs were hemmed in from all sides. The confinement of eight long months had exhausted their already small stock of provisions, not a grain being left in their store house. Famine now commenced its ravages among the besieged Sikhs and they were reduced to extremities.

At this, difference of opinion rose between Binod Singh and Banda Bahadur. It was decided that one of them should leave the place. Binod Singh accepted the decision and mounting his horse he rode out of enclosures with sword in hand and cut his way through the besiegers.[146]

Samad Khan kept on the policy of strengthening the fortification around the fortress by raising tall towers and deep moats. He sealed all the outlets from the fortress. Yet he sought blessings from every *Pir* and *Wali*. He would not think of storming the fortress (a residential *Garhi*). He was seeking some way, right or wrong, even by giving false promises to make the Sikhs surrender and come out of the fortress.[147]

In fact the entire Mughal history in India is replete with besiegement of forts. Almost all forts were taken by purchasing some of the besieged soldiers/their commanders and with their help entered the fort, occupied it with their forces. In Gurdas Nangal, it was virtually impossible to purchase a section of the

[146] *Ibid.*, p. 206.

[147] *Panjab History Conference proceedings*, Punjabi University Patiala (Seventh Session) 1972, p. 47.

Sikhs. Hence, recourse to false promises was taken up. He, therefore, adopted the only possible course of strengthening the siege and marking his time.[148]

Prolonged negotiations were carried out with the Sikhs and vague promises of their release after surrender were given, even these did not come through. Banda Bahadur offered to surrender himself on the plea that rest of the Sikhs will be released unharmed. But even that did not work. Baj Singh also offered to surrender, but that too did not find approval. At one stage, Samad Khan wanted Banda Bahadur's son and few important sardars to be sent to his court before giving any indication of what would be the final outcome.

These discussions have been summed up by Gurbaksh Singh as under:

(i) Banda Bahadur would not surrender unconditionally and that the surrender was preceded by a negotiated settlement.

(ii) According to the terms of the settlement, the Nawab promised to spare the lives of the Sikhs if they relinquished their hold over the fortress, and that the Nawab would recommend their case to the Emperor and would mediate on their behalf.

(iii) the Nawab offered these terms only 'out of expediency' and that he was not sincere in keeping his promise.

(iv) the Nawab deliberately broke his plighted word because he knew the sanguinary nature of the Emperor and he also wanted a further rise for himself in the Imperial services.[149]

The Mughal commanders decided on cutting through subterranean passages close to the gate and in this manner they

[148] *Ibid.*, p. 48.
[149] *Ibid.*, Gurbux Singh assessment, p. 59.

were able to surprise the Sikhs who were now hemmed in from all sides. The siege became so strong that it became impossible for Sikhs to bring anything from outside. Near famine conditions now prevailed. The survivors were reduced to mere skeletons. They were virtually half-dead and unable to use their muskets. It had become practically impossible for them to offer any resistance and continue defence any longer.[150] At last on Wednesday 17th December 1715, the Sikh enclosure at Gurdas Nangal, the so called fortress of Gurdaspur fell into the hands of the Mughal besiegers. The surviving Sikhs in the *ihata* had been physically incapacitated and disabled to continue the defence, but the imperialists were still benumbed with terror and they dared not enter their enclosure. Abdus Samad Khan had promised to intercede with the emperor for a free pardon for them, but when the gates were opened, the besieged including Banda Bahadur were made prisoners.[151] The Imperialists fell upon the half-dead Sikhs like hungry wolves. Abdus Samad Khan had some two or three hundred of them bound hand and foot and made over to Mughal and Tartar soldiers, who put them to the sword. The dead bodies of the Sikhs were ripped open in search of gold coins supposed to have been swallowed by them and their heads were then stuffed with hay and mounted on spears.[152]

The news of the fall of the so called fort sent by Abdus Samad Khan was reported to the emperor at Delhi on 22nd December, 1715.[153] It was by grace of God and not by wisdom or bravery,

[150]Ganda Singh, *op. cit.,* p. 210.
[151]*Ibid.,* pp. 211-212.
[152]*Ibid..,* p. 212.
[153]*Ibid..,* p. 212.

says Kamwar Khan, that this came to happen. Otherwise, it is known to everyone that the late emperor Bahadur Shah with the four royal princes and numerous commanders had made efforts to repress this rebellion, but it had been all fruitless and now that the infidels (the Sikhs) and a few thousand companions had been starved into surrender.[154]

SADHURA-LOHGARH-SITARAGARH AXIS

Banda Bahadur had secured large extent of territories in half a dozen districts of Panjab in about a year's time from his arrival in Panjab. The largest chunk thereof has been faujdari of Sirhind which was won from Mughals and its faujdar Wazir Khan captured and executed.

Bahadur Shah, the Mughal emperor, had correctly foreseen the situation, that a large Sikh rebellion near the capital city could become very detrimental to the Mughal empire. He, therefore, decided to personally move to Panjab and crush the Sikh rebellion. He mustered large number of smaller contingents of governors/faujdars from the adjoining states beside the imperial forces. The entire strength of the Mughal army was around 2 lacs horse and foot and almost the same extent of camp followers.

The Mughal forces advancing into the territory occupied by the Sikh forces did fight at a few places but from most of the places smaller detachments of Sikh army went back to either Sadhura or Lohgarh. The entire operation took about three months.

[154] *Ibid.*, p. 213.

Some entrenchments were made at Sadhura from where the Sikh forces faced Mughal imperial army. Khafi Khan says that, "The Sikhs in their faqir dress struck terror among the royal troops. The number of dead and dying of imperial troops was so large that for a time it seemed that they were losing ground. Feroze Khan Mewati and Rustam Dil Khan's armies were literally maulled by the Sikhs, but before the close of the day, a fresh army of about 50,000 Mughal troops reached and joined the battle and the Mughal army was saved of a disaster. Finding themselves in no condition to face the Mughal forces, the Sikh army retreated towards the Lohgarh fort during the night. The distance between Sadhura and Lohgarh fort is about 10 miles only. The Mughal armies also moved on to Lohgarh and after fighting for a couple of days with the besieging Mughal army, the Sikh army moved out of the Lohgarh fort and got dispersed in the nearby Haripur reserve forests. This was a strategy which Banda Bahadur does not seem to have specifically planned, but was worked out as the Mughal forces with much larger manpower were closing in on them.

Bahadur Shah moved his camp from Lohgarh to Ropar and then to Lahore where he reached on 11 August 1711 and set up his camp on the bank of river Ravi. He developed some mental ailment and died on 27/28 February, 1712.

Death of Bahadur Shah was followed by the usual struggle among his sons for the throne. Azim-us-Shan, the main contender was riding an elephant when its trunk was hit by a cannon ball and became unmanageable. It threw itself in the river Ravi where the prince and the animal were swallowed by quick sand. Ultimately Jahandar Shah eliminated his remaining brother and ascended the throne on 29th March, 1712. Ten months after ascending the throne, Jahandar Shah was defeated by Farrukh Siyar, son of Azim-us-Shan.

The period of struggle for the imperial throne and disturbed state of affairs at Lahore and Delhi from February 1712 to June 1713 was very favourable to the reestablishment of the power of the Khalsa. Banda Bahadur availed this period of disturbance and occupied Sadhura without any loss of time. After capturing Sadhura, Banda Bahadur raised a fairly strong fortress adjoining Sadhura town. He dug out a ditch around the fort, used the dug-out earth to strengthen the walls of the fort and got water filled in the ditch from a nearby canal. He also raised four towers at four corners inside the fort to be used as observation posts. The fort of Lohgarh was also occupied and repaired.

From the first ridge up to the walls of Lohgarh Banda Bahadur got constructed 52 three to four feet high defensive ridges arranged in such a manner as each ridge lent protection to the next. In this manner any assailant who intended to reach the fort had to face hostile firing from every ridge that he crossed. Banda Bahadur also chose the adjoining hill, another 400-500 feet higher than Lohgarh hill, from where he could observe the movements of the Mughal forces over the entire expanse. There is an acoustic phenomenon in that hill named Sitaragarh vis-a-vis Lohgarh fort. The spoken orders from Sitaragarh are clearly audible at Lohgarh fort and likewise the reply given from Lohgarh fort is equally audible at Sitaragarh. This phenomenon still exists at the site and it is a joy to converse with a person standing almost a kilometer away. Banda Bahadur used to stay at the top of Sitargarh hill where a small stone-lined pond for collection of water exists. There is no foundation of any building raised there. Probably he stayed there in a mud-hut.

This Sadhura-Lohgarh-Sitaragarh axis was used by Banda Bahadur in 1713-14 when a very large Mughal force under top commanders invaded the areas reoccupied by the Sikh forces with directions from Farrukh Siyar that they must finish the Sikh forces and their commanders once for all.

After reoccupying the areas under Sikh operation, Mughal forces converged on Sadhura where the Sikhs gave them a good fight and during the middle of the night left for Lohgarh because of the logistics being totally against them. The Mughal armies were more than 2 lacs fighting men whereas the Sikh army was about 20,000-30,000 only. Mughal armies followed them to Lohgarh and there again, after giving a good fight for a couple of days, the Sikh army dispersed during night time in the reserve forest of Haripur.

The Sadhura-Lohgarh axis was very effectively planned by Banda Bahadur to give a fight to a very large army and then get out of the same unscathed.

V

Massacre of Sikhs and Banda Singh Bahadur at Delhi

Banda Singh Bahadur and the other Sikh prisoners were initially taken to Lahore and then to Delhi for presentation to the Mughal Emperor. Although Banda Bahadur had been captured, imprisoned and chained, yet the dread of his supernatural powers was so haunted the minds of the Mughal commanders that every moment they were afraid of his escape. A Mughal officer offered to be tied together with Banda Bahadur on the same elephant; the idea being that if he attempted to escape the Mughal officer will plunge the dagger into his body.[1] With fetters on his feet, a ring round his neck and a chain round his back, all connected by hammer-like pieces of wood, he was thrown into an iron cage, chained to it in four places. Two Mughal officers were tied to him on each side of the same elephant to guard against his escape.[2] His officers and principal men were put in iron chains and paraded in a body mounted upon lame, worn down, mangy asses and camels and with paper caps on their heads. They were preceded by drummers and bandsmen, and Mughals carrying the heads of Sikhs on spears. Behind the prisoners were the royal amirs, fauzdars and Hindu rajas at the head of their respective troops. For miles, the *shahi*

[1]Ganda Singh, *Banda Singh Bahadur*, Amritsar, 1935, p. 214.

[2]*Ibid.*, p. 214.

sarak was lined with eager spectators on both sides and the bazaars, the streets and the roofs of the adjoining houses, presented the spectacle of a surging sea of humanity. With such a cortege of half dead prisoners and bleeding heads, Abdus Samad Khan entered the city of Lahore.[3] What a disgraceful and abominable conduct of a victorious army of the so-called civilized Mughal empire against the injured prisoners of war. Abdus Samad Khan requested for permission to present in person his great prisoner, but he was ordered to remain in his capital and send the prisoners in the charge of his son Zakariya Khan and Kamaruddin Khan.[4]

At the time of his departure from Lahore, Zakariya Khan considered the number of 200 prisoners to be too small to be presented to the emperor. He, therefore, ordered a general hunt for the Sikhs throughout the country. The faujdars and chaudharys scoured the land in search for Sikhs. Number of innocent persons were arrested from villages and sent to Zakariya Khan to make up the required number of prisoners. In a few days, large number of Sikhs having taken no part in the Sikh rebellion were arrested and only because they belonged to a non-Islamic creed, required to make a sizeable number of 740 to be butchered after Emperor's inspection at Delhi.[5]

Banda Bahadur and others, says Cunningham, were marched to Delhi with all the signs of ignominy usual with bigots, and common among barbarous or uncivilized conquerors. Like their Chief, they were put in irons, and chained in feet, waist and neck, and were loaded in twos or

[3] *Ibid.*, p. 215.
[4] *Ibid.*, p. 216.
[5] *Ibid.*, p. 217.

threes on bullock carts. At Sirhind they were paraded through the streets and exposed to the ridicule of the people who poured the filthiest language on them. The Sikhs bore these indignities with the greatest patience singing the sacred hymns of their gurus.[6]

On the 25th of February, 1716, the arrival of the prisoners at Aghrabad was reported to the Emperor at Delhi. Mohammad Amin Khan was sent by the emperor to make necessary arrangements for bringing the Sikh Chief and his followers in procession from Aghrabad to the imperial palace.

On 27th February, 1716 Banda Singh and other Sikh prisoners were conducted in a procession to the city of Delhi. The ceremonial on this occasion was copied from that observed after the capture of Maratha chief Sambhaji, son of Shivaji. First of all came the heads of 2000 executed Sikhs, stuffed with straw and mounted on bamboos. Along with them was carried at the end of a pole the dead body of a cat to show that every living creature in the enclosure of Gurdas Nangal had been destroyed. Banda Singh himself came next seated in an iron cage. The sides of the cage had large number of embedded nails with the sharp end facing towards the captive so that it would hurt him any time he put his body to a side. Behind him stood with a drawn sword in his hand, a male clad officer from the Turani Mughals.[7] After his elephant came other Sikh prisoners 740 in number tied two and two on saddle-less camels. On their heads were placed fool's caps of ridiculous shapes. One of their hands was pinned to the neck between two pieces of wood, which were held

[6] *Ibid.*, p. 217-18.

[7] *Ibid.*, p. 219.

together by iron pins. Some of the principal men, who rode near to their chief's elephant were dressed in sheep-skins with the wooly sides turned outwards. At the end of the procession rode three Mughal commanders Amin Khan representing the emperor Farrukh Siyar, Zakariya Khan and Qumr-ud-din Khan. The road from Aghrabad to Lahori gate, a distance of several miles was lined on both sides with troops and large crowds mocking at Banda Bahadur.[8]

Mirza Mohammad Harisi, who witnessed the procession, has recorded the same as an eye witness in his *Ibrat Namah*. "On this day I had gone to see the *tamasha* and accompanied the procession to the *Qilah-i-Mubarik*. Almost the entire city population had come to see the prisoners. The Musalmans could not contain themselves for the joy. But those unfortunate Sikhs, who had been reduced to this last extremity, were quite happy and contented with their fate, and not the slightest sign of dejection or humility was to be seen on their faces. In fact, as they passed along on their camels, they seemed happy and cheerful, joyfully singing the sacred hymns of their Scriptures. If any one said: "now, you will be killed", they shouted, "kill us, when were we afraid of death". Sayyed Muhammad, author of the *Tabsirat-un-*Nazirin, who was present there has stated, "Not all the insults that their enemies had inflicted could rob the brave disciples of Guru Gobind Singh of their natural dignity, without any sign of dejection or shame they rode on calm and cheerful even anxious to die the death of martyrs."[9]

Banda Singh Bahadur and other Sikh leaders were made over to Mir Atish to be imprisoned at Tripolia. The remaining 694

[8] *Ibid.*, p. 221.

[9] *Ibid.*, p. 223.

Sikhs were handed over to Sarbara Khan Kotwal for execution.[10] The Sikhs arms and valuables collected and brought by Mughal commanders for inspection of the emperor were as under:

Swords	1000
Shields	278
Bows and Quivers	173
Matchlocks	180
Daggers	114
Long Knives	217
Gold Mohars	23
Rupees	A little over 600
Gold ornaments	a few.

The list of arms taken and cash seized, remarks Irvine, does not give a very exalted notion of the military strength or the wealth of the Sikh leaders in the fortress of Gurdas Nangal. It is really astonishing that with such scanty resources, the Sikhs so determinedly resisted the greatest empire of the day for such a long time, says Kamwar Khan.[11]

The execution of Sikhs began on 15th March, 1716 opposite Chabutra Kotwali. One hundred of the Sikh prisoners were taken out of their prisons every day and were seated in lines in the Qatalgah with blacksmith kept ready in attendance on the executioners to sharpen their swords. Life was promised to every one who would renounce his faith, but they would not prove false to their Gurus and to the last it has not been found that one apostatized from their newly embraced faith, write Surman and Stephenson. The Sikhs welcomed death with undaunted spirit, presented their heads to the executioners with cheerful faces, and,

[10] *Ibid.*, p. 223.

[11] *Ibid.*, p. 224.

with the words '*Waheguru*! *Waheguru!*' on their lips, they joyfully gave up their lives amidst the wondering praise of the populace. At the time of execution, their constancy was remarkable to look at, and 'Me Deliverer! Kill me first!!!" was the joyful prayer that constantly echoed all around in the ears of the executioners.

All observers, Indian and European, says William Irvine, unite in remarking on the wonderful forbearance and resolution with which these men met their fate. Their attachment and devotion to their leader were wonderful to behold. They had no fear of death and they called the executioner 'Mukta' or the Deliverer, but what is singular, writes Ghulam Hussain Khan, the author of Siyar-ul-Muthakherin, was that these people not only behaved firmly during the execution but they would dispute and wrangle with each other for priority in execution and they entreated the executioner for the purpose. For a whole week the swords of the executioners did butcher's work and in this manner all the Sikh prisoners were beheaded. After the heads had been severed from the body, the bodies were thrown into a heap and at nightfall they were loaded in carts, taken out of the city and hung up on the trees.[12]

Many wonderful stories of the unshakable constancy and the whole-hearted devotion of the Sikh prisoners to their faith and their leader were then current. Some of them were so wonderful that those who were not eye witnesses to them were inclined to dismiss these as incredible, says Khafi Khan. But the following is recorded by him in his *Muntakhib-ul-Lubab* p. ii, 766 as 'what he saw with his own eyes'.

Among the prisoners sentenced to death was a Sikh youth of tender age. He was the only son of a widowed mother. He had

[12] *Ibid.*, p. 226.

only recently been married and as yet had the *Kangan-i-Arusi*, the marriage thread, on his wrist. Hearing of the impending doom of her son with the other prisoners, the old mother approached Ratan Chand, Diwan of the Wazir, and through his influential support, pleaded the cause of her son with great feeling and earnestness before the Emperor Farrukh Siyar and Sayyed Abdullah Khan. To avail of the Emperor's general offer to spare the lives of those who renounced the Sikh faith, the old woman, probably as tutored by Diwan Ratan Chand, represented that her son was only a prisoner in the hands of the Sikhs and was not a follower of the Gurus. He was brought here, she said, while in their captivity and now stood innocent among those condemned to death. Farrukh Siyar commiserated the old woman and sent an officer with orders to release the youth. The woman arrived with orders for the release just as the executioner was standing with the bloody sword over that young man's head. She presented the order for his release to the Kotwal. He brought out the prisoner and told him he was free. But the boy refused to be released, says Khafi Khan, and loudly cried out: "My mother is a liar. I am heart and soul a devoted follower of the *Gurus*. Send me quickly after my companions". No bewailing cries and tearful entreaties of his old mother and no persuasion of the State officers, writes the author of the *Tarikh-i-Muhammad Shahi*, could shake the young Sikh in his devotion to his faith. The spectators were further dumbfounded when the heroic boy retraced his steps back to the place of execution and calmly bowed his head before the executioner to meet his death. In an instant the executioner's sword went aloft and descended on the frail neck of the youth, and he was enrolled as one of the truest of the martyrs produced by the Sikh religion.[13]

[13]*Ibid.*, p. 228.

On 9th March, 1716, Sarbrah Khan Kotwal conveyed, under the Emperor's orders, seventeen of Banda Singh's principal men into the fort. For three months after the massacre there was a lull, and Banda Singh and his companions remained confined in the Imperial Fort. The object of this confinement and the three months' delay in the execution of the Sikh Chief and his deputies is explained in a letter, dated Delhi, the 10th March 1716, from Messrs John Surman and Edward Stephenson, the members of the English Embassy to Emperor Farrukh Siyar, to the Honourable Robert Hedges, President and Governor of Fort William."He at present", the ambassadors reported, "has his life prolonged with most of his Mutsuddys in hope to get an Account of his treasure and of those that assisted him, when afterwards he will be executed. It was not till June 19th that he was let out to execution and subjected to a death of torture."[14]

The fate reserved for Banda Singh is too excruciating to be described. On Sunday, the 19th June, 1716, "when the sun had risen about three spears on the sky", Banda Singh, his son Ajai Singh, Sardar Baj Singh, Ram Singh, Bhai Fateh Singh, Ali Singh, Gulab Singh Bakhshi and others, who had been confined in the fort of Delhi, were led out of the fort. As on the day of his entry, the Sikh Chief, laden with fetters, was dressed in a gold embroidered red turban and a robe of gold brocade. He was placed on an elephant and with twenty-six other Sikhs in chains marching behind him were taken through the streets of the old city to the shrine of Khwaja Qutab-ud-din Bakhtiyar Kaki, where the red stone Qutab Minar is located amidst white marble

[14] *Ibid.*, p. 230.

over the crumbling walls of the old Hindu fortress. Here he was paraded round the tomb of the late Emperor Bahadur Shah.[15]

After Banda Singh had been dismounted and seated on the ground, he was offered the usual choice between Islam and death. But the chosen disciple of Guru Gobind Singh chose to lay down his life as a devoted follower than to abjure his faith for the sake of enjoying a few more years of life.[17] His young son, Ajai Singh, about four years, was then placed in his arms and he was told to take the boy's life. Banda Singh refused to oblige. The executioner then hacked the child to pieces joint by joint with a long knife, dragged out his quivering heart and thrust it into the mouth of his father, who stood unmoved like a statue, completely resigned to God's Will.[16]

Amin Khan, having had the opportunity to come close and to look at Banda Singh, was surprised at the nobleness of his features, and could not help addressing him. "It is surprising", said he, "that one, who shows so much acuteness in his features and so much of nobility in his conduct, should have been guilty of such horrors". With the greatest composure, he replied: "I will tell you. Whenever men become so corrupt and wicked as to relinquish the path of equity and to abandon themselves to all kinds of excesses, then the Providence never fails to raise up a scourge like me to chastise a race so depraved; but when the measure of punishment is full then he raises up men like you to bring him to punishment".

His own turn came next. First of all his right eye was removed by the point of a butcher's knife and then his left. His left foot was cut off next, and then his two hands were severed

[15] *Ibid.*, p. 232.

[16] *Ibid.*, p. 232.

from his body. His flesh was then torn with red-hot pincers, and finally he was decapitated and hacked to pieces limb by limb. Banda Singh remained calm and serene amidst these tortures, completely resigned to the Will of God and the Guru, and died with unshaken constancy, 'glorying', says Elphinstone, "in having been raised up by God to be a scourge to the iniquities and oppressions of the age".[17] The other Sikh prisoners shared the same fate and were put to the sword.[18]

Farrukh Siyar ridiculed Baj Singh over his bravery by having been made by Mughal soldiers, incapable of doing anything. Baj Singh said, "If you remove my fetters, I will show you some *tamasha*". Emperor ordered his fetters to be removed. No sooner Baj Singh was free, he pounced like a hawk and killed two or three of the Mughal soldiers with his handcuffs before he could be apprehended and executed.

Rabindar Nath Tagore has written a highly touching poem *Bandi Bir* [Banda Bahadur] on Banda Bahadur's execution. The last stanza thereof is as under:

"All who watched were struck dumb,
Banda's body was torn to pieces,
With pincers and burning tongs,
Bit by bit, he was scorched and burnt
With unshakable courage Banda faced
A martyr's death that day,
Uttering not a single cry of pain,
All who watched stood dumb
With horror their sight was numbed."

[17] *Ibid.*, p. 234.
[18] *Ibid.*, p. 235.
[19] *Ibid.*, p. 236.

Index